TIME OUT

TIME OUT

Using Visible Pull Systems to Drive Process Improvement

WAYNE K. SMITH

John Wiley & Sons, Inc.
New York • Chichester • Weinheim • Brisbane • Singapore • Toronto

This book is printed on acid-free paper. ∞

ISBN: 0-471-19214-9

Printed in the United States of America

10 9 8 7 6 5 4 3 2 1

To my daughters, also my good friends,
Julie David and Carol Wellington.
Once I taught you, and now you teach me.
I am much better for your help and friendship.

Contents

Section 2

Organization and Metrics

Section 3

Assessing and Planning

Section 4

Pull Scheduling

Section 5

Visible Management and Continuous Improvement

Preface

Throughout this work, I'll refer to the "traditional manager." I'm very familiar with that person, because I was one for most of my Du Pont career. The story in this book is the story of my success as a traditional manager and my gradual evolution and eventual departure from that role.

I spent 32 years within the Du Pont company, covering many diverse and complex roles. Over the first 22 years of that career I worked at five manufacturing sites. In the course of that time I worked most/all of the typical plant assignments, including scheduling and inventory control, manufacturing and technical management. For 7 of the last 10 years I served as Director of Manufacturing for the Industrial Films Division. (At the time, the title was Manufacturing Manager. Since then they have upgraded the title without a change in job content, so I have granted myself that title also.)

Du Pont is a great company and has enjoyed particular success over the past few years. But now, and especially then, it is a very ingrown organization. We were proud of the fact that we promoted from within and that employment with Du Pont offered almost lifetime security. We were publicly recognized as one of the world's best-managed companies and we took great pride in that. We had a very strong and well-developed culture, and each new person who entered at the bottom of the pyramid was molded to that culture. Each learned the pattern from his or her leadership, enforced it by interactions with peers, and passed it on to subordinates. Belief in the truth of the system was validated by the successes and rewards that came from faithfully conforming.

No one from the outside ever entered the sanctuary and challenged the belief structure. (Maybe someone did, sometime, but if so, they were quickly flushed out before they could challenge seriously, because they didn't fit in.)

For much of my career I was molded by that culture and enjoyed the rewards. Everything that the traditional manager says in this book, I said. Gradually, in my later years, I began to sense that something didn't fit. In my last Du Pont years I had a chance to test some very radical approaches. At that time (1988), I had manufacturing responsibility for a film division. Our prime product was one that we had invented and for which we had held a proprietary (essentially a monopolistic) position for many years. It was a star product, growing strongly and earning company-leading margin and return. But by 1988 we had lost our patent, and competition (Japanese) was emerging. After many years of arrogance, we were suddenly *very* concerned about our competitive position.

That, incidentally, is typical of Du Pont. We were world class in terms of research and product development. We invented cellophane, nylon, Teflon®, and so on. With those inventions, we established new markets and enjoyed great successes, *until* we had to deal with competition and operating in a commodity instead of a monopolistic environment. Our film product was a classic example of that problem.

To challenge and revise our strategies, I had commissioned a "Greenfield" committee. The members' charge was to think out what we would do, if we had the opportunity to start completely over ... in a green field. They were to open up their minds, forget convention, and find new ways of looking at our business.

That committee was having trouble breaking out of the box, and as I searched for ways to help them change their paradigms, I heard about an experiment in a "cycle time" approach to management and improvement that the Corporate Manufacturing Committee was considering.

That experiment was to test the concepts that had previously delivered so much success in the discrete parts industry. ("Just-In-Time [JIT]," "Toyota Production System," "Continuous Flow Manufacturing [CFM]," and "Pull Scheduling" are various labels for the same basic idea of evaluating an operation from the standpoint of the time captured within the operation.) Those ideas had produced a revolution in the screw-nut-bolt-assembly arena but had not been successful in our chemical or process industry. The experiments were to be small, and they were being done as much to disprove as to prove the concepts.

As I learned more about the concepts and the intent to test, I became strongly convinced of the merits in that approach and wanted to be involved. For the first time in my career, I essentially browbeat the committee into appointing me as the manager of that experiment.

I remember sitting with the VP-Chairman, who said, "I understand you want to be the Cycle Time Manager?"

"Jack, who do you want me to kill?" was my reply.

I'm always taken by how lives can turn upside down as a result of tiny incidents; my life certainly changed immeasurably at that moment.

As we conducted those first pilots, the results were beyond all expectations. Benefits were different than expected, came earlier, had more far-ranging effects, and changed the very culture of the plants involved. All of a sudden, our small team was faced with a demand across all of global Du Pont—140 sites in 29 geographic regions.

Over the next three years we followed a strategy of implementing in selected core plants and then using the expertise gained within that site to lead projects in associated sister plants. In that way, we were able to grow geometrically by transplanting knowledge. (I will stress repeatedly in this book that you can't appreciate or make full use of these principles until you have lived through an actual implementation. You have to *see* the elephant before you can appreciate what an elephant is.) After three years we had touched some 80 sites, and total benefits that third year (1991) exceeded $100 million.

I left Du Pont in 1991 to work more broadly in learning and teaching cycle time methods. In so doing, I have been the prime beneficiary; I have learned more about the keys to managing and improving a work process in the past 7 years than I learned in the entire preceding 31 years.

My only wish is that I could somehow go back in time and redo those years with the benefit of what I've learned over these past few years. I don't get that opportunity but, through this book, you *do* get the opportunity to avoid those mistakes in the first place. This book is the distillation of those 38 years and a complete road map of the final methodology.

Acknowledgments

Although this work may be identified as the product of one author, it is truly the combined efforts of many. I have been on a journey for almost 10 years, and in the course of my work I have interacted with hundreds of people: authors and consultants who have laid the foundation, coworkers and collaborators who have worked with me through the discovery process, and, most important, the users of this process who have both contributed to the process and have validated it through their successes. Without all of those, this work would not exist.

Of particular note: IBM Consulting who provided my introduction to cycle time strategies. Spectrum Management who first noted the distinction between convergence and divergence; the critical distinction that suggested to me why cycle time had not been successful in the process industry and thereby pointed the way to some of the special adaptations in this book. My original Du Pont cycle time team (John New, Lew Buckminster, Larry Mlinac, Steve Kempton, Paul Veenema, and Pete King) who did the initial Du Pont implementations and formulated the first drafts of this process. Courageous early clients who provided a laboratory for me, including Reg Geck at Union Carbide, Alex Kwader and Pete Gendreau at Specialty Paperboard, Ron Saporita at W. R. Grace, Greg Bialy at Rohm & Haas, Alan Goodman at

ISP, and Oscar Saldarriaga at Jafra Cosmetics. Tricia Moody, editor of *Target* magazine, who encouraged me to undertake this project. Finally, my wife Linda, for the environment of support she provides.

I am deeply grateful for the association with each of these people. My license plate is LVNLRN (this is the first of many tests in this book) and these people have made both objectives possible. If this book makes a contribution, it comes on their shoulders.

SECTION 1

Making the Decision

Time is the most important resource ...
It is the only one that cannot be recovered.

—*Henry Ford, 1928*

CHAPTER 1

An Overview

Introduction

Perhaps because I've spent my life involved in it, I consider the manufacturing discipline to be a high calling. All our goods and services come from manufacturing. Our position in the global economy is largely determined by our manufacturing capability. Most innovation is born by the desire to compete and succeed. Consider the pocket calculators we take so much for granted. When I studied engineering at the University of Michigan, all engineering students were marked by the slide rules they carried for doing calculations. The best and most prized, made of bamboo and having (perhaps) 20 scales for doing exotic logarithmic work, cost about $40. With no advance in technology and with normal inflation, that slide rule today would cost more than $200. Yet a fine pocket calculator with business and statistical functions can be had for a fraction of that amount. The drive for manufacturing excellence and financial success has delivered that benefit to us all.

Literally millions of people in this country derive their very welfare from the manufacturing sector. Moreover, they derive meaning and purpose of life from their effort; more waking hours are spent in the execution of their job than any other activity.

If manufacturing is that fundamental to our lives and welfare, we had better do it well! This book is about that, performing the manufacturing function well, and continuing to learn how to do it better.

We're going to do that by trying to make a complex subject appear to be simple. It isn't! But if we can learn how to recognize the few really critical considerations, if we can make those considerations visible to everyone, and if we can focus or concentrate on doing those few things excellently, then we will have made complexity and difficulty to appear *as though* they were simple.

One of the primary points of this book is that success is tied to rigorously following a methodical process. My usual experience is that people try to do too much, that they are not careful about what is critical, and that they therefore don't do anything with any degree of excellence. Little wonder that the bottom line doesn't change.

This book lays out the details of the process that I have found effective, and it does that in depth; nothing will be held back. Your first impulse may be to scan through the chapters, pick out the specifics that excite you, and charge out to do only those. *Please resist!* To help your discipline and understanding, the process is broken into five logical segments that provide the structure of this book:

1. **Making the Decision.** This involves a high-level view of the entire process. It is a road map showing where the process will lead, the resource requirements, and a method for estimating what benefits you might expect. After reading this section you should have a good basis for deciding whether to dive in.
2. **Organization and Metrics.** Establish the direction, metrics, and guiding organization for a Time project.
3. **Assessing and Planning.** Identify opportunities for improvement by mapping and modeling. Assess opportunities, choose Time tools, and condense the assessment into a specific plan for change.
4. **Pull Scheduling.** The primary tool in managing time in a process is a Pull System. Unique adaptations and special methods result in successful application within your specific environment.

5. **Visible Management and Continuous Improvement.** Use the base provided by Pull Systems to institute an ongoing and focused continuous improvement process. Build employee involvement through employee empowerment. This section ends with an overall Time Benchmark to continually measure your organization's evolving capabilities, to compare your company to world-class organizations, and to guide your ongoing growth.

Each section includes all the specifics you need, and each ends with a detailed checklist of tasks to be completed before moving on. I firmly believe that you'll maximize your final result if you force yourself to move faithfully through each segment, completing each before you step into the next.

So What? Why Should I Care?

Right now, you may be wondering "Why should I bother to read this? What's in it for me?" To answer that, I'll give you a very high level view of what you can expect to experience if you meticulously follow the road map that this book lays out.

1. You will reorganize a portion of your global business team into a cycle time Steering Team. That team will do the following:
   - Revisit the critical business issues
   - Define strategy and revise performance metrics in support of that strategy (The metrics-setting effort is a first key; metrics will guide and measure the detailed execution.)
   - Identify a four- to eight-person full-time cycle time Core Team
   - Provide for Core Team facilities
   - Meet periodically (every 2–4 weeks) to monitor, guide, and facilitate Core Team work
2. The Core Team will spend two to three months analyzing the operation on the basis of time trapped in the operation and non-

value activities required by the operation. They will develop a Change Plan (including costs and benefits) and present that to the Steering Team. You will gain few benefits (if any) during this period.

3. Assuming the Steering Team approves the Change Plan, the Core Team will require about two to three months to implement those changes. The changes will be shop floor changes aimed at stabilizing, simplifying, integrating, and optimizing the daily operation. Objectives will be in inventory control, capacity optimization, customer service, and quality. You will get only minor benefits during this period—"low hanging fruit" that you can pluck easily and quickly, without interfering with the main project.

4. Upon implementation, you can expect benefits to flow back rapidly and surprisingly. As every implementation is different, specific benefits can't be projected for your case, but with my experience over many implementations, I find the following to be typical benefits:

Capacity:	10%–20% Gain (by bottleneck optimization)
Inventory:	30%–40% Reductions
Cycle Time:	50% Reduction
Quality:	5%–15% Increase in Final Yield
	2× to 10× Increase in 1st Pass Yield
Service:	Improved Lead-Times and/or On-Time %

Said another way:

$ Benefits 1st Year: 2X–30X project resource costs

Some of these benefits will be onetime inventory reductions. Many will be continuing benefits that will roll in every year.

5. At the end of that five- to six-month effort, you will be in a continuous focused improvement mode, extracting waste and time from your process based on information flowing up from an involved and empowered workforce ... forever. (Cycle time is not a onetime project that is completed from which you move on. It is an ongoing and continuous process for improving the process incrementally by *ruthlessly* extracting time from it. This implementation will set you up to pick fruit every day!)

If all that sounds appealing to you ... please read on.

Why Haven't I Seen This? (Why Breakthrough Improvement Doesn't Happen)

I contend throughout this book that these techniques are revolutionary, that true breakthrough improvement can result from disciplined application. If that is true, the old question—"If you're so smart, why aren't you rich?"—surely applies. Or, more directly, if these ideas are so powerful, why isn't everybody using them? The answer is that a number of very powerful inhibitors must be overcome. Among them are the following:

- The power of the paradigm
- Traditional metrics: traditional behavior
- Issues of power and control

Power of the Paradigm

Dr. Joel Barker[1] has published extensively on the subject of *paradigms*, the rules or models that we use to understand and to work with our surroundings and environment. He (and others) have observed that our personal paradigms are so powerful that, when confronted by evidence that our paradigms are wrong, that evidence can be invisible to us. The classic example is the Swiss watch industry. It totally dominated the world watch market when a Swiss researcher invented the quartz watch. As it did not have hands, jewels, a mainspring, and so on, Swiss watch management literally did not recognize the invention as a watch and exhibited the invention publicly as a curiosity *without patenting*. As a result, within three years the industry had lost some 75 percent of its market and its employment. The industry was devastated by the power of its own paradigm about watches.

The same thing applies to our vision of what constitutes informed management of manufacturing processes. We all have succeeded by applying a certain set of rules. As we have achieved success, these rules have become indelibly written into our set of management paradigms. In the case of senior management, this imprinting process has gone on for more than 30 years. For them to change is to suggest that their 30-year investment has been wrong. (Note: It is *not* a matter of right or wrong. As long as everyone has the same set of paradigms, everyone is safe. As soon as one company adopts a new and better paradigm, the whole world changes.)

Throughout these discussions, our key words are going to include terms such as *simple, visual, manual, shop floor, common sense, real-time,* and *employee driven.* These concepts can be in stark contrast to MRP,[2] SQC,[3] SPC,[4] QFD,[5] TPM,[6] MIS[7] or computer-driven anything, and centralized anything. A paradigm conflict results, and the security of people involved in any aspect of modern management is threatened. A *major* objective of this book is to show that a cycle time strategy is not in conflict with any aspect of modern management sciences.

As we discuss application of these concepts, the stepwise process that begins with senior management is intended to avoid the paradigm problem. Starting this process on the shop floor will not produce permanent sustainable change, because unaltered senior management paradigms will lead to management behavior that will effectively cancel changes as they happen. This in turn will cause the shop floor to revert to practices that are in harmony with management paradigms. See Section 2 for more information on senior management's role in a cycle time project.

Metrics and Behavior

Dealing with the *metrics* that we use to manage our processes is actually a specific part of the paradigm problem. We all grew up (as managers) with a traditional (BAU, or "Business As Usual") set of performance metrics. We have succeeded by applying those metrics; they are a powerful way to describe what constitutes good manufacturing performance. Some of them are shown in Box 1.1.

Please don't chuck this book immediately when I suggest to you that all those cherished metrics from your own past *may very well be wrong* in today's environment. That is one of the reasons why you don't see these concepts in application: You'll have to give up (or at least alter significantly) those old measures in order to adopt a cycle time approach.

As we work through the sections of this book, I'll suggest a new set of base measures. Among them are those shown in Box 1.2. (Throughout the book, *quality* will refer to product quality, and *Quality* will refer to quality in everything done for the customer [recognizing that everyone has a direct customer, in addition to the business's end paying customer].)

If you compare the following two lists of metrics, I think the contrast should be obvious. Many of the BAU metrics encourage production (whether you need it or not) and/or discourage idle time. More production means labor content per unit or fixed cost per unit will be

---

Box 1.1 Traditional (BAU) Metrics

- Cost per unit of production
- Labor per unit of production (lower is better)
- Production total per accounting period (higher is better)
- Fixed cost per unit of production
- Capacity utilization (higher is better)
- Idle time (idle is bad)
- Inventory (inventory as an *asset*)
- Capacity impact of transitions, or campaign length (long runs maximize capacity and protect manufacturing from sales demand variations)
- Capacity of a production unit or line (bigger, wider, more powerful is better—BAU)

Box 1.2   Time Metrics

- Cycle Time (Ct). The time it takes material to move from raw material through the process and ultimately to the customer. Cycle Time is inventory expressed in terms of days of supply; the formula is inventory in the system divided by daily demand for that inventory.
- Value-Add Time (Vt). The portion of Ct for which the customer has value and for which he or she would gladly pay.
- Manufacturing Cycle Efficiency (MCE = (Vt/Ct) · 100). This is a measure of how much waste is trapped in your process. If you are from the process industry and you haven't done your homework, I'll bet your MCE is 1% or less!
- Capability Index (Cp). How robust is the process? The ratio of product quality variability vs. Customer Spec width. This is a Quality classic.
- 1st Pass Yield. The percentage of material that goes all the way through *the first time* without reject or rework.
- Takt Rate. "Takt" is German for beat of the music and "Takt Rate" is the integrated pace at which all process steps are to run (units of production per unit of time).
- Lead Time (Lt). The time interval between order receipt and promised delivery of product.
- On-Time %. The delivery performance against quoted Lead Time.
- Bottleneck Efficiency: Utilization of the bottleneck relative to the theoretical maximum. A measure of the "leakage" or inefficiency of the critical step in the process. Per Eli Goldratt in *The Goal*[8] ... if you optimize the bottleneck, you optimize the entire process.
- Market Share %. There are two ways to improve Ct: Drive inventory down *or* move more product.
- Capacity Utilization. I contend that this number can get too close to 100%.

lower, idle time is reduced only by making more, capacity impact of transitions can be reduced most easily simply by making longer runs (which acts to increase total amount made), big, wide, high-capacity production units (which are greatly desired by traditional managers) need to justify their high investment by pumping out the product ... and so on.

Note what happens when metrics encourage overproduction. If I am a supplier to you, and if I produce faster than you consume, then material piles up between us. As material piles up, each unit of material waits longer (or moves slower). In that condition, assume that I make something that is bad. Several undesirable results occur:

- It will be a long time before you find that bad unit.
- When you find it, you won't care (because you have a large pile of available material to choose from).
- When you find it, I don't care (because I made that last Tuesday and certainly am not doing that now).

The effect is that we are disconnected; cause-and-effect relationships between the two stations will be invisible. If, however, I make something only as you need it, then if I make something that is bad, you will see it immediately; you will throw it back at me, and I have nothing to do except respond to the problem. We are connected; cause-and-effect relationships are obvious. *My contention is that BAU metrics encourage disconnection.*

However, under our Time strategy, the primary metric is Cycle Time—the time it takes material to enter, move through the operation, become a finished product, and ship to the customer (and perhaps also until the customer sends back payment). The classic formula is inventory in the system divided by the output demand for that material: $Ct = \text{Inventory/Demand}$. Note: As manager of an operation, you can't reduce your Ct by simply shoving material downstream; it has to be *demanded* by your downstream customer. Hence, inventory that you are responsible for is your work-in-process (WIP) plus all downstream inventory until that material is actually drawn into the downstream operation. My conventional symbology includes a circle to represent an operation, an arrow to represent a transport, and a triangle to represent a storage point (see Figure 1.1).

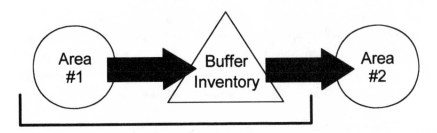

Figure 1.1 Responsibility for Cycle Time Extends Downstream

The basic premise of a cycle time strategy is that we want to minimize Cycle Time, to understand the reasons for buffer inventory, to minimize inventory (numerator in the Ct formula), to maximize output demand (denominator of the Ct formula), and to balance production between stations (to ensure that I supply to you at a rate equal to your consumption so that the pile between us doesn't get bigger). We'll go into great lengths as to how to do that, but part of it is resisting the traditional impulse of emphasizing production and avoiding idle time.

This section is titled "Metrics and Behavior." The connection between the two is that metrics *determine* behavior; people perform according to how they believe they are measured. Therefore, if you want to change behavior, you must start by changing metrics. Said another way, any spontaneous change in shop floor behavior will be canceled if it is in conflict with management metrics. Traditional BAU metrics are a powerful paradigm because they are the way we in senior management gained our success. According to the paradigm principle, any evidence that suggests that our paradigms are wrong will be invisible to us. Hence, adopting cycle time behavior requires first accepting cycle time metrics and that is very threatening to those of us who have a conflicting history. (See Section 2 for a complete discussion of metrics.)

> "You tell me how you're going to measure me ... I'll tell you how I'm going to perform."
>
> —Eli Goldratt

Issues of Power and Control

The dynamics of an organization are dominated by issues of power and control; to many of us, power and control are synonymous with success. Cycle time strategy threatens or redefines power and control in any number of ways. Two examples follow.

1. Continuous Improvement. An essential part of this approach is the concept of continuous *incremental* improvement. Traditional management approaches improvement from the top down; management identifies and drives improvement opportunities. This book presents a method that starts with capture of detractors on the shop floor and then funnels the major problems upward for resourcing by management. That approach is based on the fact that if you want to involve people, you have to empower them. If you want to empower people, you have to give them the tools/methods to determine or control their own destiny or future.

2. Scheduling. A fundamental of cycle time strategy is *Pull Scheduling*. A full section is devoted to that subject, but basically Pull is a technique for managing/scheduling the daily shop floor activity by the shop floor people. The prime objective is to link workstations so that each produces in rhythm with and in response to its downstream customer demand to avoid the pileup of material and disconnects. The concept is that it is impossible for a remote agency to respond/react to the minute-by-minute changes that occur, around the clock, on the shop floor. Pull is a mechanism that gives the floor the means for reacting instantly and almost automatically to any unexpected deviations. That is in stark contrast to the MRP approach of using centralized and powerful computer systems for scheduling. Most large organizations now include central MRP organizations charged with scheduling, inventory control, and customer distribution and service. Those organizations can be very threatened by any suggestion that scheduling is going to shift toward the shop floor people: It is a basic issue of power and control.

A later section shows that these Time concepts are not in conflict with MRP, that instituting Pull Scheduling on the shop floor frees MRP and empowers MRP to provide the long-term management perspective that is critical to long-range health and success. To implement cycle time concepts, issues of power and control must be addressed.

Summary: If This Is So Good, Why Don't I See More of It?

- Power of the Paradigm. Cycle time strategy conflicts with the good management rules we have learned as we have succeeded.
- Metrics. To change behavior, we must first change the things we value and measure; these new metrics are counter to our traditional metrics.
- Power/Control. Before implementing cycle time concepts, we must resolve issues of power and control that threaten those very people who must drive the implementation.

CHAPTER 2
The Foundation for Cycle Time

Philosophy

Although this book lays out a work process and/or a collection of tools and techniques, cycle time is first a basic philosophy distinctly different from the approach that has guided industry throughout the modern era. Therefore, implementation cannot begin with physical changes on the shop floor, and in fact cannot begin at the operating levels of the organization. Cycle time is nothing more than a fundamental culture change and must begin at the very core of the organization. Several basic points of philosophy are the starting points:

- There is a direct connection between the *Quality* of a process and the *time* that is trapped in it.
- Behavior at every level is determined by the performance metrics applied to that level. People perform according to how they believe they are measured,
- A critical aspect of management is the ability to *focus*.
- *Incremental* improvement is more powerful than a "big bang" approach.

QUALITY AND TIME

"Big Q" Quality is defined by the customer—Quality is meeting/ exceeding all expectations without waste activities that the customer does not value. "Customer" is whoever you supply: the paying customer at the end of the value chain or the next workstation in the manufacturing process.

The Quality/time connection occurs at two levels in a continuing cycle of improvement. First, if the objective is to reduce time, the only way to begin to do that is by learning how to do only right things, and to do them right the first time. (This is the basis of our analysis process.) As you do that, waste activities are eliminated and inventory piles get smaller, and that results in materials moving faster to the receiving station. As that happens, the stations become more closely coupled and cause/effect relationships become more obvious. As the supplying station then responds to those more visible needs, a second round of improvement and time reduction occurs.

That cyclic process of learning how to go faster *because of* going faster continues forever, a never-ending journey.

METRICS AND BEHAVIOR (REPRISE)

I've already introduced this idea in Chapter 1: People perform according to how they believe they are measured (see Box 2.1). Several points are important:

- This is not a matter of how you *say* they are to be measured; it is how they actually *are* measured. Or, said another way, *informal* metrics are much more important than *formal* metrics. The questions you ask and the attitudes you display when you are out on the floor have more impact than the reports that the floor people are required to submit. People are very sensitive and intuitive concerning what is really important to management.
- If you wish to change behavior, you must first change metrics. Or a change in metrics must result in a change in behavior.
- If you see behavior that concerns you, you must look inward at the way you are signaling to the organization.

Box 2.1   A Metrics Example

I did some work with a precious metals fabricator that consisted of three manufacturing areas: melt shop, rolling mill, and fabrication. The manufacturing manager's primary metric was dollar volume shipped by each area by month.

The behavior that we observed was as follows:

- The last week of the month was an intentional crisis; volume averaged 50% of the monthly total, with 30% overtime. The union considered that overtime to be their right, or entitlement.
- Volume in the first week of the month, after all orders had been pulled ahead, averaged 15% of monthly volume while people stood around with little to do.
- No attention was paid to ship dates. Each area reached out and grabbed the highest dollar-volume order in the queue.
- No attention was paid to quality. "I know that's going to come back, but ship it anyway."
- On-time delivery performance was 65%.
- Each area dumped material back to the preceding area at the end of each month. Each area did what it could to sabotage other-area competitors.

The manager felt that there was great value in the excitement and thrill of accomplishment in the big month-end push.

Our recommendation was to consider the behavioral change that would result if On-Time % was to become the prime metric.

FOCUS

Everywhere I go, one of the universal failings that I see is people/organizations trying to do too much, and not completely succeeding at anything. In a manufacturing operation, any dummy can find something to work on; opportunities are everywhere, all over the floor to

---

Box 2.2   A Focus Analogy

The focus concept is like chasing rabbits in a field. If you try to chase every rabbit, you'll never catch any. The better way is to pick out the biggest, fattest, slowest rabbit, chase it, catch it, kill it, and eat it—and then look around for the next one to chase.

---

trip over and raining down upon everyone. The skill is in determining *what* to work on and to then *stay* working on that item until it is complete (see Box 2.2).

A prime benefit of pursuing a Time strategy is that it allows you, or *forces* you, to focus. If the objective is to go faster, or reduce Cycle Time, you must be alert to those things that slow movement and correct/improve them.

Closely related to the idea of focus is the idea of *integration*. In most/all organizations, you will find competing ideas or concepts, each trying to be *the* central driving methodology. Competing ideas waste energy and damage one another, when in fact all may be able to play a significant role. With a Time approach, all those arguments go away. If our objective is to extract time from the operation, one segment of the operation might need to focus on scheduling, another might need to apply SPC to improve yield, another might need TPM to improve machine reliability, one might need QFD and Six Sigma[9] to improve customer quality satisfaction, and so on. Although each segment might appear to be different, all are doing what they individually need to do to extract time. The umbrella of Time allows one integrated analysis, followed by an unemotional selection of the specific tool that each particular operation needs. Cycle time analysis integrates all the various "alphabet soup" tools that confuse us all.

After decades of observing and managing manufacturing operations, I am convinced that if you can identify the one thing that will have the biggest impact on cycle time, that is the one right thing to do. Conversely, when I am considering alternative projects, if something under consideration does not have significant impact on time, I'm simply not going to consider that alternative.

My consistent observation is that organizations tend to do too much. In a later section, we'll talk extensively about project management skills. That complex subject breaks down to some simple skills:

- Analyzing alternatives based on their impact on Cycle Time (finding the fat rabbits)
- Severely limiting what the organization attempts to undertake
- Once opportunities have been targeted, not allowing a change of mind (churning priorities is a good way to never catch a rabbit)
- Using basic project management accountability—assigning specific names to specific rabbits and committing to when they will be stew

INCREMENTAL IMPROVEMENT

In my Du Pont experience, we loved to talk about "order of magnitude change," "leap-frogging" the competition, and "hitting home runs." When we conducted our experiments with Time strategies, however, we learned that high value for home runs is wrong. There are always all kinds of incremental improvement items just laying around waiting to be picked up. When we did pick them up, we were surprised to see that the combined impact of small items every day was more by far than the impact of an infrequent home run, and we were shocked to see that some of those items were in fact home runs. We didn't have a good way of evaluating what their true impact would be, and we hadn't been picking them up because they were not what management valued; we therefore didn't see connections between these small/easy improvements and our individual career advancement.

Generally, these incremental items had to do with removing a nonvalue activity, removing some waste, reducing wait time, or in some way making things move more smoothly, freely, or quickly. When we did that, we moved into the improvement spiral I mentioned earlier that is driven by making cause-effect relations clearer by making stations more closely connected.

This experience led to a complete reversal of our priorities; we came to value improving in the *quickest* way possible instead of the *biggest* way possible. A Time strategy is a strategy of a bunt single every day: Move the runners along, score a single run every chance you get. Let the competition swing for the fences; they'll hit one out every now and then and be very happy on their way to second place.

Principles of Operation

This philosophical base leads to or supports four fundamental principles used in implementation and operation of a Time strategy:

1. Total quality
2. Elimination of waste
3. Operator involvement
4. Balanced production

TOTAL QUALITY

The intent here is Total Quality in everything that you do for your customer, whoever that customer is. The principle of providing Big Q Quality means that customer expectations must be known, documented as specifications, those specs must be linked to process parameters that influence performance against those specs, and that your process for meeting those specs must be in control.

The means for delivering Quality is by implementing the following principles.

ELIMINATION OF WASTE

The way to deliver a positive is to eliminate all possible negatives. This principle says that we are going to examine everything we do in terms of what the customer values. Anything that the customer does not

---

Box 2.3   Waste?

Waiting	Sorting
Testing	Transportation
Counting	Reworking

---

value, that she or he would not *gladly* pay for, is defined as waste and is a target for elimination.

By that definition, a (partial) list of waste examples is shown in Box 2.3. People generally have trouble with defining the following two categories as waste.

Transportation: You have to get the product to the customer; how can transportation be considered waste? This question introduces the concept of *essential* as opposed to *waste*. An action may be essential, but not necessarily of value.

Consider the possibility that you have two alternative products you are considering for purchase. One was made right in your own community, and one was produced 1,000 miles away. Would you pay more for the product that must be shipped in? Of course not. You might even be willing to pay more for the item produced locally (since you would have easy access to the producer for service). Therefore, although transportation may be necessary or essential, it does not add any value.

Testing: Certainly testing your product to ensure its quality is adding value. Right? Wrong! This is again confusing essential with value. Activities may very well be essential without adding value (see Box 2.4).

Consider this: Assume that I have two widgets for you to choose from. I assure you that either is good, but one has had extensive testing. Question: Would you pay more for the one that has been tested? That is not a hypothetical question. When you buy a VCR from Sony, take it home, and turn it on, that is the first time it has been turned on. Sony didn't test it; they *know* it is going to work, because their quality is that good. Now, assume you heard that Sony had just instituted a broad quality testing program. What would you think? You would wonder why that was necessary and would assume that Sony had lost con-

---

Box 2.4   Testing: Value or Nonvalue?

When Honda ships cars from Japan, they are shipped without gas in the tank. That is not because Honda drains the gas before loading them in the boat; that is because they don't start the engine at the factory!

Honda is the premier producer of internal combustion engines, and they are in control of their manufacturing process. Testing more would not add any value.

---

trol of quality. Would you pay more to support the cost of that testing? No, you would not, and you would probably elect to purchase another brand.

Eliminating waste is at the core of a Time methodology process. We'll talk extensively about mapping the process to understand where waste is located and then working incrementally to methodically root waste out and to prevent its return.

OPERATOR INVOLVEMENT

The only way to approach an objective as broad as attacking all waste is to involve the entire organization. At Du Pont, we had made a number of attempts at operator involvement in the 1980s. As we attempted to flatten the organization and downsize the corporation, we recognized that we would need the contributions of our shop floor personnel. But for decades we had effectively told them to "park your brains at the door . . . we'll tell you what to do and how to do it." We had very effectively told them that participation in management or improvement was not their job or responsibility.

The involvement programs we attempted failed, in my opinion, because we communicated new philosophy without method; we told people *what* we wanted from them but not *how* to do it. Our classic example was when we attempted to introduce the concepts of TQM. We held classes in TQM and insisted that TQM activities should be

In Du Pont's experience with Time strategies, the major benefit was the empowerment/involvement of the shop floor personnel by means of the simple, visual, manual, operator-owned tools implemented by floor people.

reported each month, but when people left the classroom and asked "What am I supposed *to do?*" we told them to find something that didn't work well (that was "broken") and to just fix it. The point is ... *we didn't know what was broken!* Further, if we knew something was broken, we did not have a good way to know its connection to the whole. It is certainly possible to improve something that will have no bottom-line impact. Better capacity on a nonbottleneck step, for example, will not result in a single additional widget produced. If we had not allowed individual initiative before, and if we didn't know what needed to be fixed, how could we possibly expect our people to know how to respond?

A Time approach is different; it starts on the shop floor by capturing information about what adds to Cycle Time. It provides floor operators with tools to allow them to participate in the improvement process by initiating it. Management does not decide what is to be fixed, they resource what is funneled to them.

The moral here is that if you want to involve people, you must empower people. That is what this process does; it provides tools on the floor, *for* the floor, so that employees have some control of their own destiny.

BALANCED PRODUCTION

BAU management values production. If you have your downstream customer buried in product, you are succeeding. But we've already talked about the problems of disconnection. If I run faster than you can consume and bury you with WIP (work-in-process), then each unit of material moves slowly and we become disconnected. With that comes loss of understanding about cause and effect. Also, local optimization (behaving to maximize my individual performance numbers) becomes the norm. I cannot act to benefit the whole, because I cannot see my impact on the whole.

To avoid disconnection, our objective is *balanced production*. That does not mean equal capacity at each station (that is neither possible or even desirable). It does mean that all stations run at the same pace (our term is *takt*, to the same beat of the music). The tool for achieving balance production is *Pull Scheduling*.[10]

Pull is the absolute guts of a Time implementation; all of Section 4 is devoted to the subject. Here the concept is briefly introduced.

To understand Pull, you must first understand its alternate and predecessor, "Push" Scheduling. Classical Push is the way American industry has always scheduled. A business generates a sales forecast and converts that into an area-by-area production schedule. Each area then runs as hard as it can against that schedule and *pushes* material forward. Excesses and disconnection result.

Excesses also generate waste or nonvalue activity; as that material piles up we need space to store it, we need people to put it away, we need to account for it, some material will go bad or become obsolete while in storage so we'll need to test it later, we'll need some just-in-case (JIC) extra inventory, and so on. All those inventory-associated activities are waste!

In contrast, Pull Systems act to limit and control production based on downstream demand. Like many other of the techniques in this process, Pull is simple, visual, common sense, pencil and paper, operator owned.

In the JIT revolution that swept the auto industry and ultimately all discrete parts production in the 1980s, Pull Systems were a cornerstone, and the techniques are well documented. Almost no one has made the transition to implementing Pull in process (diverging) industries. The major barriers to Pull are posed by divergence (multiple choices for what to produce), by long and difficult transitions, and by the inability to start up or shut down process equipment quickly. The subject of Pull is too rich to cover in this brief overview, but here are a few questions to pique your interest.

• Continuous process operations like to run products in a regular repeating product sequence—a *product wheel*. BAU manufacturing likes to turn this wheel as slowly as possible to minimize the impacts of transitions and to isolate the operation from the turbu-lence of the market. But doesn't that imply excess production?

- How do I know exactly how long the production sequences should be?
- If I could time the product wheel exactly, and therefore knew when I would be back to a product again, wouldn't I know exactly how much intervening inventory I would need? (No, you wouldn't ... until you also know the type of customer service you want to pro-vide downstream.)
- What is the importance of knowing the bottleneck step?
- Do I service the customer order from a Finished Product Ware-house? From the end of the production line? From somewhere within the process? Do I care?
- How does all this relate to MRP? Are Pull and MRP redundant or competitive?
- What is the right capacity utilization percentage? How much do I load my equipment up before thinking of expansion? How does this relate to customer service? To inventory management? Do I care?

Do you know how to answer these questions? By the end of this book, you will.

Values: Business as Usual versus Time

The end result of adopting a Time philosophy and acting according to Time principles is that the organization comes to hold different values. The value contrast is illustrated in Box 2.5. The following paragraphs discuss some of the issues in Box 2.5.

BIG VERSUS SMALL

There are two traps in the question of capacity; the first is that bigger is better. The conventional wisdom is that big, wide, fast, high capacity is

Box 2.5 Organizational Values

BAU	Time
Production	Reduced Waste
Cost	Time
Area Performance	The Whole
Competition	Optimize Bottleneck
High Capacity	Smaller Units?
Flexible	Inflexible?
Minimum Idle Time	Avoid Excesses

good; labor cost per unit of production is minimized and cost performance is therefore better.

A true story: I was once part of a Du Pont business team responsible for a high-tech product that we had invented and for which we held patent protection; we enjoyed a global monopoly. Our process featured a huge production unit that produced all product variations and serviced the world. When we lost our patent protection, a Japanese competitor began offering very limited quantities for one specialized and narrow market from a small pilot production unit. We laughed: "That's a joke. Wait until they have to compete in the real world."

Question: When they filled that small unit with sales, what do you suppose they did? Answer: They built another unit just like the first, picked out another market segment, and filled that with business. The eventual result was a number of units, each of which produced continuously for a special market segment while we attempted to serve all masters with our massive unit. Result: We got killed!

The second capacity trap is the assumption that it's best to run flat out, to fully utilize capacity. After all, doesn't that spread fixed cost and give minimum total cost? Since this issue is too complex for this section, please refer to Section 4 and the discussion of product wheels. The basic idea is that when you get to capacity extremes, you have no reserve capability to respond to any unexpected detractor. When something unexpected and negative happens, there is no way you can catch up until something randomly positive happens to put you back on track. Once management understands this issue, they will understand the need to hold some reserve capacity for smoothing out the bumps.

FLEXIBLE VERSUS INFLEXIBLE

This is the same question as the preceding. In the interests of being highly flexible, a unit can lose significant efficiency to transitional downtime and to poor quality as a result of continual change. If particular products can be assigned and constrained to specific production units, those losses may not be necessary. This concept attacks the closely held management paradigm that flexibility is to be valued and instead suggests that you can sometimes greatly simplify your operation by being *inflexible*.

In discrete parts, the old school approach was to group similar machines together (the drilling department, the milling department, the grinding department, etc.) and to route parts through the departments. This is referred to as the *farm* layout (peas here, carrots there . . .). That was replaced under a Time strategy with *cellular* manufacturing, where all machines needed to produce a particular part or assembly were grouped in one location (the carburetor cell, the engine block cell . . .). Cellular layouts had a tremendous time and inventory advantage over farm layouts.

The process of limiting and controlling the number of alternative routes that a specific model, grade, or product type may take through the larger plant is the process industry equivalent of cellular manufacturing. The strategy was originally referred to as *Group Technology*, but I now refer to it as *Virtual Work Cells* as that more accurately depicts the intent: We are managing specific routes through the plant *as though* the equipment within that route were grouped into a cell. See Chapter 3 for a brief discussion and Section 3 for more details.

COMPETITION VERSUS THE WHOLE

The traditional style of management is to measure performance by area and to therefore, intentionally or not, pit one area against another in "healthy" competition. (Refer to my analogy in Chapter 1 of the plant that measured performance in terms of shipment by area.) The mistaken idea is that if each area performs to the max, then the system will also perform to the max. In his book *The Goal*, author Eli Goldratt has powerfully shown that any system has a single definitive bottleneck and that the entire system cannot do better than that bottleneck. It makes sense, then, that the full organization should pay attention to and defer to the bottleneck. In contrast, traditional competition encourages defeating the bottleneck or, at the least, pouring energy into things that don't do anything to further the bottleneck—classical "waste" activity.

The intent, then, in a Time strategy is to concentrate on the bottleneck. The problem is that traditional systems don't provide a way for an individual or a workstation to even *see* their effect on the bottleneck. That is one of the main purposes of Pull Scheduling, discussed in detail in Section 4.

CHAPTER 3

A Process Overview

The purpose of this first section is to give you the information you need in order to decide whether a cycle time implementation will benefit your operation. So that you have some view of what is involved in conducting a full cycle time project, a brief overview of the steps detailed in Sections 2 through 5 is presented here. Note: This brief discussion is no adequate substitute for the detail in the following segments.

What I am about to describe is not rocket science. Some of the concepts are new (Pull adaptations for the process industry, for example), but many are well known. Individually, each technique is not particularly difficult or abstract. In fact, special value is given to tools that are easily understood and used directly on the shop floor. Anything that can't be explained to the floor doesn't belong in a Time toolbox.

What *is* special is the method for implementing these ideas. Incorporated in this book is a specific road map, and adherence to that road map allows the many component techniques to function in a synergistic way that is not possible when those tools are used in isolation. The ideas are simple but are decidedly not easy! Applying them requires rigor and discipline, and to adopt this process one must give up some very closely held beliefs.

Organization and Metrics

Section 2 deals with getting organized and setting direction for a cycle time effort. The basic premise is shown in Box 3.1. It follows, then, that the activity must be initiated and guided by a global Steering Team (perhaps a special function of the existing business team). That team includes positions such as the business manager (profit responsibility), sales manager, marketing manager, manufacturing manager, the manager of scheduling and distribution, and the manager of engineering or research.

The first function of the Steering Team is to revisit business mission or vision, reassess critical success factors, and set metrics for the business and for this cycle time activity (these should be the same). In that metrics-setting process, the team is careful to consider *all* stakeholders: the customer, the stockholder, the employee, the community, environment, innovation, and so on. The intent is to define the entire business environment or playing field, to identify the four extreme corners, and to be balanced and strong in all. I refer to this as a *Four Corner*[11] method. Further, the Steering Team makes careful distinction between *strategic* (where do we want to go?) and *tactical* (how are we going to get there?) metrics. Tactics determine shop floor activity. I have observed that business teams spend too little time on setting

---

Box 3.1

Basic Premise

A cycle time process must be business driven and must have clear business objectives.

Corollary

The process cannot be seen as a manufacturing activity with manufacturing or local optimization objectives.

strategy and far too much time dictating tactics to the shop floor (when they are too removed from the shop floor to know what the best tactic in each part of the factory truly is).

With strategy and metrics in place, the Steering Team then establishes the cycle time Core Team. This may be one team that is active through implementation, or it may be one team that does the analysis and planning portion of the task and another that does full implementation.

An issue associated with teams is whether to use full-time or part-time teams. With the downsizing and flattening that everyone is doing, no one has capable resources waiting in the wings to take on this type of task. Therefore, everyone always wants to do this with part-time teams. My position is that, if absolutely necessary, the part-time option can be taken. But consider the information presented in Box 3.2.

The Core Team will consist of a leader (communication, team, and project management skills plus high visibility and credibility are important), representatives from areas likely to be affected (manufacturing areas, maintenance, scheduling), plus at least one person with technical or data analysis skills. When we began forming these teams at Du Pont, we put high value on technical skills and university degrees (that is a common failing in Du Pont). As we progressed, we learned that many of the team members could and should be hourly employees. Further, that team is often expanded in the implementation phase with hourly people to *ensure* that the details of implementation are planned and executed by the shop floor. You don't really get shop floor buy-in if the plans are dictated to the floor.

Throughout the project, the Steering Team serves to set direction, to receive recommendations from the Core Team, to set priorities, and

---

Box 3.2   Resourcing the Process

- With part-time teams, the process will take *four times as long,* and will deliver *half the benefits.*
- I have never seen a full-time team that did not deliver more benefits in the first year than the resource costs.

to facilitate the implementation. *It does not problem solve or dictate actions.*

Assessing and Planning (Identifying Opportunity)

Once direction has been set and performance metrics have been established, the first active step is to understand "where are we now." The Steering Team has established a goal or objective and, just like any other journey, you can't possibly get there unless you know where you are starting from.

MAPPING

That discovery process is a mapping process. There are three types of maps: an *operations* map, a *Cycle Time* map, and a *Management Process*[12] map.

The operations map is just that, a diagram that shows all that happens to material as it moves from the raw material pile through the manufacturing process into the distribution chain and ultimately to the final customer. Creating the map involves agreeing on some standard symbols for types of operations; ideally those symbols should distinguish between those that add value and those that do not. The process is aided by thinking of that process as progressive flybys. The first pass is done at very high levels and only major blocks can be seen. With agreement on what those blocks are, another flyby is done at lower levels, adding more detail. Ultimately, the plane is little more than a crop duster, and every significant detail is visible.

While we're distinguishing between value-add and waste, we're also distinguishing between essential and nonessential. What we would like to find are activities that are both nonvalue and also nonessential. When we find those, we don't do them anymore (and time in the process is extracted). See Section 3 for an understanding of why non-value and nonessential activities would exist in the first place.

More likely, we'll find nonvalue work that is currently essential. *That is an opportunity*. If we can find a way to convert essential to nonessential, we can eliminate and speed up. Again, see Section 3.

A Cycle Time map is quite different. Remember, the definition of Cycle Time is Ct = Inventory/Demand. A Cycle Time map is nothing more than a layout of the plant showing the location of all inventory, expressed in terms of days of supply. Analyzing the map in terms of *why* that inventory needs to be there in that quantity and playing What If games around how the size of the piles could be reduced will produce many improvement opportunity ideas.

Sometimes, the underlying reason for inventory, and for waste activity, is the business or management processes used. People can get so accustomed to a cushion of inventory that it becomes a self-fulfilling prophecy—"Why do you have three days of inventory here?" "I don't know, just because." A cumbersome quality release procedure can cause material to pile up at the Quality Control (QC) lab. Or a desire to self-protect against delay can encourage extra inventory (maybe even unreported extra inventory!). A Management Process map deals with that. A three-level map of the management methods looks at the *planning* process, the *execution* process, and—positioned between the two—the *control* process. Control interfaces between the original plan and the shop floor results, and either adjusts floor activity to achieve the plan or signals the planning function that the plan is no longer viable. The control function is very often where a Time project needs to work in order to drive out waste and time. And, in keeping with our basic philosophy, we encourage control mechanisms that are simple, visual, shop floor, operator owned, real time, and so on. See Section 3 for more discussion.

Each of these mapping activities will generate a lot of questions, such as "Why do we do it that way?" and "Why couldn't we ... ?" At this point, the idea is to just capture the ideas, not to filter or process the ideas. Even if you don't know how to do something, if it is just something that you would like to be able to do, capture it. "Capturing" usually means writing it on chart paper and taping it on the wall. In this phase, teams literally paper the walls with opportunities. Three hundred to four hundred opportunities are typical; the world record to my knowledge is 1,100 opportunities at one particular plant site of about 800 people.

Mapping became an integrating tool in Du Pont. When we began our Time effort, there were many other improvement efforts—TQM, Total Productive Maintenance, Quality Function Deployment, Time To Market, SPC, Process Control and Automation, and so on. Proponents of each competed with one another, shouted that they had the Holy Grail, threw rocks at one another. We finally realized that all those efforts began with something like a mapping activity. We were able to convince all parties that if we did *one* map for each work process, that map in some cases would point to maintenance as critical, in some cases would point to statistical quality, in some to scheduling and inventory, and so on. If we approached each business together, we would not compete, we would not confuse the business, and all disciplines would have more work than we could possibly do. That integrated process in Du Pont is now referred to as the Continuous Business Improvement Process.

MODELING

A parallel activity to mapping is *simulation modeling*, the process of building a computer simulation of the manufacturing process. Simulation used to be a very unlikely option; software was very expensive ($15,000–$20,000) and required skilled programmers to build the model. Now, effective and economical ($1,000) simulation software packages[13] are available that will run on your desktop PC (or even your laptop), and no special programming knowledge is required to use them.

Modeling is an optional and not essential part of the analysis phase. But there are two strong reasons to consider modeling:

1. To confirm understanding of the process. If your model does not reflect real life, then you don't understand real life. Almost always, when a firm builds a model of its operation, the model runs better than real life—better yields, higher capacity, lower inventory, better customer service, and so on. That is not because the model is

wrong, but because things are happening in real life on the shop floor that don't show up in the operations manuals. To get the model to reflect reality, it is necessary to go out and dig around and find the leaks that have not been built into the model. As you find those leaks, they suggest opportunities for improvement that you would not have considered if you had not modeled.

2. To play "what if" about the future. Once you have a model of the current state, and after you have built a long list of opportunities, those opportunities can be tested by inserting the change in the model and observing the outcome.

For example, I worked with a polyethylene resin producer that had essentially a two-step process, a large reactor that fed multiple finishing extruders. When I first observed the process, the practice was to work very hard at minimizing in-plant work-in-process (WIP) inventory. As a result, the company never had exactly the intermediate that was needed when it was needed, so the second step in the process necessarily made finished product from whatever was available and pushed that into finished inventory. The feeling was that the company would eventually sell whatever it made.

When we mapped inventory, we saw little/no WIP inventory and *huge* inventories of finished product. My argument was that the producer should run the first step so that it always had at least a minimum amount of every intermediate, so that finished product needed for orders could always be made. My contention was that that approach would result in significant (millions of dollars) of reduction in total inventory.

The problem was that it would be necessary to build adequate intermediate inventory before the finished product pile could be reduced, and that buildup required an up-front inventory investment of millions of dollars before the company would recoup the savings. Understandably, management was reluctant to change their approach to scheduling and to invest that capital, without proof that the new approach would work.

The resolution was that we modeled the new approach and gave management confidence that they could undertake the change with assurance that they were safe.

ASSESSING AND PLANNING

The end product of the mapping/modeling stage is that the team has literally papered the walls, having generated hundreds (even thousands) of opportunities.

The key ground rule during opportunity generation is to *not filter*. All ideas are good ideas, big or small, and feasibility is not questioned. If we would like to be able to do something, but don't know how to do it, it still goes onto the opportunity list.

But I've said that one of the benefits and/or objectives of this process is *focus*, to chase only the fat rabbits. How then do we convert hundreds or thousands of opportunities into a few juicy, fat rabbits? The answer is the Seven Management Tools.[14] Most of us are familiar with the Seven Quality Tools[15] (sometimes known as Deming Quality Tools). Those are simple pencil-and-paper tools for analyzing and managing quality. The Management Tools are similar—simple, common-sense, back-of-the-envelope tools for formulating and managing programs. They are listed in Box 3.3. We won't go into the process here, but the end result of applying the Management Tools is that the team is able to pare the list of opportunities down to the few opportunities that will have major impact, and to create a process for assignability, accountability, and for tracking/monitoring progress as the rabbits are chased, killed, and eaten.

Box 3.3   The Seven Management Tools

---

1. Affinity Diagrams
2. Relationship Diagrams
3. Program Planning Charts
4. Problem/Prevention Charts
5. Arrow (PERT) Diagrams
6. and 7.   Matrix Diagrams (Two types)

Time Tools

In addition to pruning the opportunity list, there are standard Time tools that may be chosen for implementation. It is not a given that all tools will be used in all implementations, but most tools appear in most implementations (see Box 3.4). Sections 3 and 4 detail these tools. The following discussion will suffice here.

PULL SCHEDULING

This is the key to scheduling, inventory control, problem identification, bottleneck optimization, and operator involvement—*the* fundamental technique for managing the shop floor under cycle time. Pull Systems, which link stations together so that they produce in rhythm, usually have three features: limited and controlled inventory, visible demand signals between stations, and management alarms or signals when the system drifts off of plan. Pull exhibits simple, visual, operator-owned tools that operate in real time on the floor. Section 4 provides all the details for designing, implementing, and operating a Pull System.

Box 3.4 Time Implementation Tools

- Pull Scheduling
- Group Technology
- Visible Management
- Robust Process Development
- Continuous Improvement

GROUP TECHNOLOGY
(VIRTUAL WORK CELLS)

This time tool controls/minimizes the alternative number of routes that a specific product may take through a multistation process.[16] It reduces quality variation, transitional losses, and schedule churn by *reducing* flexibility.

VISIBLE MANAGEMENT

This is not making management more visible (although that will happen also). It is making *problems* more visible, so that they may be resolved more efficiently in real time on the shop floor by shop floor people. This is also the basic tool for initiating your continuous improvement system.[17]

ROBUST PROCESS

This methodology relates customer need to process variability. It is essentially the Deming type of management process aimed at process reliability. The prime metric is Capability Index: Cp equates the width of the product specification to the demonstrated product quality variability.

In old, traditional Du Pont, our great strength was the invention of new products. As we did that, we built and operated a pilot plant, and the quality output of the plant was measured. The plant capability then became the quality standard, and we transmitted that to the customer. "Mr. Customer, this is Polymer X, our new invention. It has a viscosity of 2000 centipoise and a tensile strength of 20,000 psi, and the variation on each spec is no more than plus/minus 5%. Let us know how much you want to buy." By definition, our specs were equal to our measured output and therefore our Cp = 1. Further, what do you suppose we did if/when we improved the process and narrowed the quality variation? Right! We tightened the spec and proudly told the customer. We had quarterly spec review meetings *looking* for the opportunity to tighten up. Cp = 1 was guaranteed; we managed so as to keep it so.

What's wrong with that? We made our best product, worked at making it better, and gave that improvement to the customer in the form of tightened specs. What is wrong is that:

- The specs have no correlation to what the customer might want or need.
- A Cp equal to one guarantees that there will be yield loss. After you have carefully measured the process quality output and set the specs, all processes will have long-term variation. There is no firm rule, but processes that have quality variation with a normal distribution and a Cp set to unity will typically have a yield loss of about 7%. You are the victim of your own process variation. And yield loss means waste: inspection, rework, just-in-case inventory, and so on.

The better way is to start by determining the true customer need. That establishes meaningful specs that then can be left alone while quality improvement narrows the variation. The objective is to achieve a Cp equal to two, product variation that is half of the specification. In that circumstance, typical yield loss is essentially zero, 3 ppm. You are bulletproof to variation.

A continuous management process is employed to tie QC specifications back to process control parameters, to identify causes of variation, to do root cause, and to ensure permanent elimination or improvement. The first stage of that process is to establish SQC: measurement, control, and reaction to measured product quality. This describes management of quality in or by the QC lab, where quality is measured. The end state is to implement SPC, where tight statistical control of the process guarantees that product quality is also in control. This is management of quality on the shop floor where quality is created.

CONTINUOUS IMPROVEMENT

Everything that comes before is done to reach this phase. Once in place, this tool is used forever. In this sense, the methods in this book do not describe a project but a process. This is a never-ending journey that goes on forever. It is the continuing process of identifying detractors, reducing those detractors to their root cause, selecting for impact, focusing on the critical few, and effecting permanent elimination through use of good project management skills. Conducting continuous improvement requires reconstructing the management process—the schedule, agenda, and conduct of the regular management meetings. Whereas the traditional management process has always been initiated and driven from the top down, this process is initiated upward by the shop floor and is then resourced or facilitated by management. This becomes the basis for employee involvement. What I have continually seen is that to involve the shop floor, one has to empower the shop floor. That means giving them tools to manage their own environment, to control their own destiny. The continuous improvement process is that tool.

Understanding Inventory

When managers are exposed to Time strategies, they tend to focus on the benefit of reduced inventory. Inventory gains are an important part of cycle time, but inventory needs to be put into perspective. Box 3.5 contains some important points.

Box 3.5 Managing and Reducing Inventory

- Inventory is there for a reason. It is there to float you over some problem or limitation that you have either not recognized or are not able to fix.
- Management edicts to reduce inventory will not work if the underlying problem is not removed.
- However, if the problem is removed, you don't have to worry about removing the inventory; it vaporizes spontaneously!

I think we've all been through the experience of being directed to "cut inventories 20% by the end of the year." We do that; we incur customer service or efficiency penalties; and inventory comes right back after New Year's. That is because we did nothing to change the basic capability of the system. In fact, the original impetus for these strategies came from exactly that experience. The people involved in one such failed experiment realized that successful inventory management had to involve understanding and changing how the basic underlying process worked. Moral: Focus not on the inventory, but on the *reason* that it is there!

Defining Process Industry

We have said that a Time management process will apply anywhere, to a manufacturing process or to a white-collar paperwork process. Within the manufacturing process, it applies to any type of manufacturing process.

But these ideas originated in the discrete parts industries, the screw-nut-bolt, fab and assembly operations. Most noticeably, these ideas emerged from the auto industry and the supporting parts suppliers. Because of that history, there is a lot of doubt about application in the process industry. I refer to that doubt as the "We're Different" syndrome, which is expressed something like this: "Thank you very much for telling me all this. It is very interesting and I've learned a lot. But ... let me tell you why we're different and why this won't work in my case." I want to make two points: that this process works *anywhere* and that, specifically, it *does* work in the process industry.

But, first, what do we mean by "process industry"? When you examine specific factories, you'll find that none fit a precise description. First, there is a confusing mix of terms: process, discrete, continuous, assembly, and so on. Second, no plant is exclusively of one type; there are aspects of discrete in continuous operations and vice versa (continuous operations produce discrete unit package quantities such as bags, drums, tank cars, etc., and discrete operations make large batch runs that approach or simulate a continuous operation).

I've found that a much better definition is *converging* or *diverging* industries.[18] Conventional discrete operations where these ideas originated are converging operations—thousands of parts are assembled down into one car. Typical process industries (steel, paper, film, food, etc.) diverge—few raw materials are run through standard process steps to produce a wide variety of finished SKUs (Stock Keeping Units). So in this book, when I talk about process industry, I mean *diverging* operations.

Diverging operations have unique problems. At every divergence point, once you commit resources to a specific branch, you can't reverse that decision. That is why, in an environment where production is valued whether it is immediately needed or not, management often finds themselves with tons of material in finished inventory while they are unable to meet today's due orders. Also, divergence poses special problems when trying to install Pull Scheduling. That is why you don't hear much about Pull or JIT, nor do you see kanbans, in process plants. I'll discuss that at length in Section 4.

CHAPTER 4

How Will We Know When We're Done?

This is how each section of this book ends, with a list of things that should be accomplished before moving on. I believe it's important that you be rigorous about this: Do the work in each section completely and well before moving on.

This book describes a process. It can't be taken apart, you can't decide to do only the parts that appeal to you, and you can't do them out of sequence. (Of course, you *can*; you just won't get the benefits that you should, and the improvements may not stick.)

Often, I have seen projects rushed through critical steps so as to get more quickly to the bottom line, only to collapse or retreat because important early foundations were not laid solidly. It's almost tragic to talk to a company that has taken years to drive its business into a ditch but is impatient about taking three months to find a way out. Equally tragic is the company that has decimated its organization through downsizing in search of a quick cost fix or stock price hype and then laments that it doesn't have anyone to assign to a team that could provide the company solutions that deliver real and sustainable competitive advantage.

A primary feature of this book is to provide a detailed process and to enforce the discipline necessary to use that process and to obtain the benefits offered.

So, for this first section, here are the things you should do before moving to Section 2, "Organization and Metrics." Note: For all of the estimates required below, do only a rough estimate. Hip-shot numbers are all that are required to know whether you should do this or not. *Do not waste any effort on decimal accuracy.* The team that you form will do the more accurate version and as Time disciples, we're not into waste/duplicate activity.

A "Do List" for This Segment

1. Every member of the business team should read this section.

2. Estimate Cycle Time (Ct—the time it takes a unit of production to move from raw material through the process, become a finished product, and finally ship to the customer). This is basically converting inventory quantities into days of supply. The important point is that it must be *all* inventory—no exclusions. Estimates include held stock, technical stock, rework, and so on. This can be done one of two ways: Each inventory pile can be looked at in terms of demand for that pile, or each pile can be converted into finished product equivalent and then compared to demand for finished product. For example, because of yields, an inventory of an intermediate might convert to much less in terms of finished product. When that inventory is expressed in terms of days, it must be either the full pile divided by demand for that intermediate, or it must be that amount converted to equivalent finished product divided by demand for finished product. The same issue applies when you are looking at ingredients that get combined to make a finished product. Bottom line: We're tabulating inventory in terms of days of supply.

3. Estimate Value-Add Time (Vt), the time required to do only those things that truly add value to the finished product. It is the time you have your hands on the product and are actually changing it in a

way the customer values. As we discussed, this excludes waiting, testing, sorting, counting, reworking, transporting, and so on. In the process industry, it is raw process time, the time actually required to make a batch, to wind a roll, to move from input to output of a continuous reactor, and so on. In a continuous process, you'll have a problem deciding when to start and stop the clock. Visualize, for example, a steel rolling mill. A molecule may move from start to finish in seconds—is travel time of that molecule equal to the value-add time? That definition would be unrealistically severe. My convention is that value-add time is the time required to make an identifiable batch or lot. For example, the time to complete a roll of paper through a coating tower (with no time for downtime or off-quality) would be my definition of coating value-add time.

4. Estimate or identify customer order Lead Time (Lt). When I call you and place an order, what is the interval of time you promise for delivery? But be careful of finished product warehouse situations. If you ship to the customer immediately from a distribution warehouse, but the plant takes 30 days to respond to an order from the warehouse, don't say that Lead Time is zero.

5. Identify market share percentage. If not 100%, what limits increasing that market share? Are you limited by capacity of your plant (you're sold out), or is your access to the market limited by some aspect of your performance (you're not sold out and you don't have 100% share)?

6. What is our customer service performance; what percentage of product is delivered on time, when we say we will deliver?

7. What is the 1st Pass Yield? This is the percentage of product that passes all the way through the process the first time without rework. 1st Pass Yield for the full process is the product of 1st Pass Yield at each individual station. (Three stations each with 90% 1st Pass Yield have a total 1st Pass Yield of 72.9%.) Be ruthless in your estimate. If something is not exactly right the first time, 1st Pass Yield gets no credit. For example, if you mix a batch, take a color sample, and then make a final "hit" to get it just right, you've failed the 1st Pass criteria. (Section 2 covers this metric in detail.)

8. Estimate your % capacity utilization. What percentage of full capacity are you currently using?

9. Ask whether you are absolutely sure that you know what your bottleneck step is.

10. After doing all of the preceding, ask the following questions:

- What is our Manufacturing Cycle Efficiency (MCE)? MCE is equal to Vt/Ct and is a measure of how much waste is trapped in your operation. I suspect you'll be shocked at how low your MCE is. There is no general answer as to what constitutes a good MCE, but anything less than 10% is a strong signal that you have opportunity for improvement.

- Is Ct significantly greater that Lt? The more Ct exceeds Lt, the more dependent you are on forecasts, and the more inaccurate your forecasts will be.

- Does Ct indicate excessive inventory?

- What does inventory cost? Any reduction in inventory provides a onetime capital benefit as we do not have to replace that inventory. But also there is a continuing inventory carrying cost benefit. It is obvious that one benefit is the continuing cost of money; I can benefit annually through interest savings because of the capital that I have freed up. But inventory costs every year also include cost of space, labor to handle, accounting, shrinkage, and obsolescence. If my inventory is liquid in a tank, if I can inventory simply by reading a level gauge, if there are no losses, then my annual inventory carrying cost may be as low as 20%. If, on the other hand, my inventory is in the form of 50-pound bags, if they must be handled and inventoried manually, if there is a lot of bag breakage and product spoilage or obsolescence, then my carrying cost may approach 40% annually.

- Can I gain market share if I can find additional capacity? There is no more powerful way to add to the bottom line than by adding to market share. Since you already have equipment and labor in place, your cost to produce those additional pounds may be no more than additional raw materials. (Note: Don't accept that your market is fully penetrated. Markets are limited only by your definition of the market!)

- Can I gain share through customer service, price/cost, or through quality?
- Am I shocked by 1st Pass Yield?
- Do we have a significant portion of people expediting or fire-fighting? What if we could redirect a portion toward long-term development or improvement items?
- The more Cycle Time exceeds the customer order Lead Time, the more you are dependent on forecasts (and the more inaccurate the forecast will be). The *only* way to improve forecast accuracy is to reduce Cycle Time.
- The gap between Cycle Time and Value-Add Time is the measure of waste activity trapped in the process (see Figure 4.1). I'll make a bet: If you are a process manufacturer, your Cycle Time is *at least* 20 times your Value-Add Time.

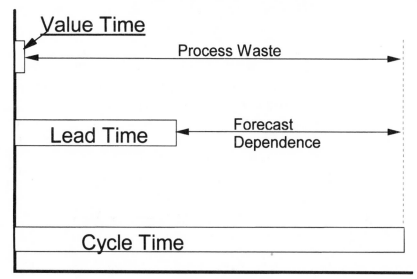

Figure 4.1 Displaying Cycle Time Performance

Estimating Benefits

After making all the preceding estimates of your current performance levels, I'm going to give you some methods for estimating the dollar benefits that might result from executing a cycle time project. Please look on this as the *grossest* of estimates, plus or minus 50%.

Benefit possibilities fall into three categories: reduction in inventory (expressed in terms of potential improvement in MCE), increase in market share, and better utilization of people (note that I *did not* say head-count reduction).

INVENTORY REDUCTION

In the previous section you made an estimate of your own MCE (Ct compared with Vt). We're going to attempt to compare your current state to world class, and then use that to get at potential for inventory reduction. To do that, we need to identify the type of manufacturing that you are engaged in, as MCE performance varies with manufacturing type (see Figure 4.2). The categories are:

Type #1—Discrete Assembly. No parts manufacture (machining, stamping, etc.) occurs; parts are assembled into a final product. An auto assembly line is the typical example.

Type #2—Mechanical Job Shop. Examples would be a general purpose machine shop, a stamping mill, an injection molding operation, a gun manufacturer, and so on.

Type #3—Batch Chemical (or Semicontinuous). Paper/film/steel manufacture, industrial chemicals, paints.

Type #4—Continuous Chemical. Refining, petrochemicals, basic high-volume chemicals, resins, and so on.

MCEs are inherently higher in discrete parts than in continuous processes. Toyota claims MCEs approaching 40% in their assembly operations, while I have seen many process operations with MCEs

MCE Multipliers

	≤5%	5%-10%	10%-15%	15%-20%	20-25%	25-30%	>30%
TYPE 1	5	4	3	2	1.5	1.3	1.2
TYPE 2	4	3	2.5	1.7	1.3	1	1
TYPE 3	3	2.5	2	1.3	1	1	1
TYPE 4	2	1.5	1.2	1	1	1	1

Figure 4.2 Leverage to Improve MCE

below 1% and have never seen a process operation greater than 10%. From that, we can make some estimate of what your potential might be based on where you currently are. As an example, if you are a machine job shop with an MCE of 12% (pretty poor), my guess is that you might expect to drive that to 12 (2.5) = 30 with concentrated effort. A continuous chemical esterification process with an MCE of 8% might hope for 12%.

What does this mean in terms of potential for inventory reductions? Remember the formulas:

Ct = Inventory/Demand
Vt = Time spent in activities that the customer values
MCE % = $(Vt/Ct)100$

Therefore:

Inventory = Vt (Demand) $\cdot$ 100 / MCE

As Vt is always a constant, and as this estimate does not deal with increasing sales, the improvement relates entirely to inventory reduction. If we estimate that our MCE multiplier is 1.5, then our new inventory level will be 1/1.5 or 2/3 of the old, a 33% improvement. A multiplier of 2 implies inventory reduction of 50%, a multiplier of 1.2 relates to a reduction of 17%, and so on.

Inventory reduction carries two different monetary benefits. As you consume inventory that does not have to be replaced, there is a

---

Box 4.1   Inventory Carrying Costs

Type #1 — 20%
Type #2 — 27%
Type #3 — 33%
Type #4 — 40%

---

onetime cash flow avoidance. Consume $1 of inventory and you avoid $1 in cash flow (once only).

But the ongoing carrying cost of inventory is also involved. If I have a dollar invested in inventory, I don't have that dollar in the bank, and I lose the interest that I could have earned. Or I don't have that dollar to invest in capital projects, and I lose the return that the project would have earned. The *conservative* estimate of inventory carrying cost is the cost of money, say 10% to 12%. But carrying cost is really much more than that. If I have inventory, I need space to put it away, I need people to handle the inventory, I need to account for it, some of the inventory will become obsolete or damaged, and so on. So the *true* cost of carrying inventory is the cost of money *plus* all the costs incurred in handling and caring for that inventory. If you have inven-

---

Worksheet 4.1   Inventory Benefits Estimate

---

1. Manufacturing Category: Type # _____
2. Inventory $ Value: $ _____
3. Current MCE: _____
4. Potential MCE Multiplier   _____
   (from Figure 4.2)
5. % Reduction (1-(1/Multiplier))   _____ %
6. One time Cash Flow Benefit (#2)·(#5) $ _____
7. Carrying Cost %   _____
   (from Box 4.1)
8. Annual Carrying Cost Benefit (#6)·(#7) $ _____

tory stored in bags, if those bags can break, if I have to manually handle that inventory to count it, if the material can spoil or become obsolete, then the full annual cost of carrying that inventory can be as high as 40% of the face value. On the other extreme, if your inventory is liquid in a tank, if all I have to do to take inventory is to read the gauge on the side of the tank, if the material never spoils, then the total carrying costs may be as low as 20%.

So use the four manufacturing categories we discussed earlier to bracket your inventory carrying costs (see Box 4.1 and Worksheet 4.1).

MARKET SHARE GAIN

The first question is: "What is my *true* market share?" Eli Goldratt (*The Goal*) says that markets are unlimited—limited only by your definition of what/where your market is. If you sell buggy whips, you might think your market is very limited. But you could look at your market globally instead of regionally. If that still limits, you might redefine your market as "horse accessories." If that limits, perhaps your market is "leather goods." (See Section 2 for a broader discussion of the importance of driving for growth, including quotes from some of industries most influential current leaders.)

With those ground rules in mind, I'm not going to allow market share estimates above 80%. If you *truly* have that type of global market share, then probably you don't have significant potential for improvement. (Even then, you might go through the following exercise on the basis of share that you may lose if you don't remain strong in the emerging competitive environment.)

Figure 4.3 provides an estimate of share gain you might experience if you pursue cycle time improvement. The table will be controversial! Current capacity utilization appears across the top of the table and current (newly and rigorously defined) market share down the side. As an example, if you are at 75% capacity utilization and 75% share, the implication is that you might capture 2.2% more through following this program.

The obvious question concerning this table is that the estimate of gain *goes up* with higher capacity utilization. The closer you are to the

% Capacity Utilization

	<70%	70-75%	76-80%	81-85%	86-90%	91-95%	>95%
80-100%	0	0	0	0	0	0	0
60 - 80%	2	2.2	2.4	2.6	2.8	2.9	3
40 - 60%	3	3.5	4	4.5	5	5.5	6
<40%	4	5	6	7	8	9	10

Market Share

Figure 4.3 Estimating Potential Market Share Gains

peg, the more I'm saying you can gain. There are multiple reasons for that claim:

- When one feels they're at capacity, marketing efforts are constrained. Sales become a self-fulfilling prophecy.
- When at capacity, operation becomes very unstable. Any mistake or interruption is catastrophic and unrecoverable. Service becomes unreliable. Customers are not happy.

Worksheet 4.2   Share Gain Estimate

---

1. Annual Sales Volume _____ units
2. Market Share % _____
3. Capacity Utilization % _____
4. Potential Increase % (Fig 4.3) _____
5. Potential Volume Increase _____ units (# 1)·(#4)
6. Selling Price $ _____ /unit
7. Variable Cost $ _____ /unit
   (Cost of producing one additional unit of production)
8. Incremental Earnings (#6 – #7) $ _____ /unit
9. Incremental Earnings Potential $ _____
   (#5)·(#8)

- Most organizations *think* they understand and manage their bottleneck; very few really do. When I hear someone say they are at capacity, I suspect there is potential for easy gains.

As a result, I'm suggesting that opportunity for share gains increase with lower share *and* also increase with high capacity utilization.

Using the share gain estimate provided by Figure 4.3, use Worksheet 4.2 to translate that gain into potential increase in earnings. (Note: The leverage here is very strong because everything necessary to produce the additional product is already in place. All that is necessary is to provide additional raw material; everything else is already paid for.)

EMPLOYEE UTILIZATION

The last area for potential improvement is employee utilization. First, let me tell you what we are *not* talking about; we're not talking headcount reduction.

I frequently talk with companies that have desperate operating problems but blanch when I suggest that they need to assign people to resolving those problems. "We don't have anyone free to do that ... we've just gone through downsizing!" Figure 4.4 illustrates what they are saying.

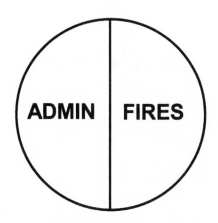

Figure 4.4 Typical Management Environment

Figure 4.5 Trying to "Drive" Improvement

All organizations divide their efforts between two types of activities: routine "administrivia" and unexpected problems. When one tries to impose improvements, to introduce change, the model looks like Figure 4.5. As one tries to drive in a wedge of improvement, no matter how world class the intent, the pressures of everyday life try to push back. No permanent change occurs.

What is needed is to first provide some tiny slice of the organization that is free to be accountable for change. (If I am first accountable for what happens on floor in this minute, I am always going to be sure that what *does* happen protects me. I'll *never* have the time or courage to devote effort in the hope that I'll make tomorrow better.)

Once that initial improvement segment is in place, those people can begin to implement improvements that reduce the fires. As fires are reduced, people are available to drive yet *more* improvements, the improvement wedge grows, and the cycle continues to free people for improvement (see Figure 4.6). Question: Do we *ever* not need further improvement?

What we're talking about in this segment is being able to free people from fires, so that they might address real and permanent improve-

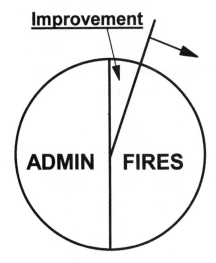

Figure 4.6 "Growing" Improvement from Inside

ment. The basis of our improvement estimate comes from a Du Pont paradigm around technical/research/management positions. Our assumption was that people in that category should be able to deliver permanent improvements (cost reduction or revenue increases) *at least* equal to the annual cost for their services—salary plus all benefits.

The "work" here (see Worksheet 4.3) is estimating for the average salary employee how much time is spent on the administrivia (left) side of our model and how much is spent on the fire fighting (right) side. My guess is that 30% to 50% is typical. Once you have made that estimate, my experience says that we can reduce that by 20% through the process described in this book, and that the people who are freed up cost us $100,000 annually (including all benefits) and that they can provide permanent benefits equal to their cost. That's a lot of estimates, but I'm confident that they are conservative!

PROJECT COSTS

The preceding will have projected some very significant benefits. But they don't come without the expense of commissioning a full-time

Worksheet 4.3   Utilization of People

1. # of salary roll employees   _____
2. % of time spent on fire fighting   _____ %
    (Overall average)
3. # of people fire-fighting (#1)·(#2)   _____
4. Potential reduction (#3/5)   _____
    (Assumed 20% reduction in fires)
5. Potential 1st year benefit (#4 × $100K) $ _____

Worksheet 4.4   Cost of the Effort

1. # of major production areas   _____
2. Core Team size (#1 + 4 people)   _____
    (Addition of Maintenance, Scheduling, Q/C, and Leader)
3. Man-years ((#2/2) +1)   _____
    (Team for 6 months plus 2 follow-up for 6 months)
4. Annual Cost (#3 · $100,000) $ _____

team for six months, with a smaller follow-up team active for a further six months (see Worksheet 4.4).

Summary:
Is This Worth the Effort?

In Worksheet 4.5, we've summed our benefits estimates, compared them with the cost, and developed a return rate. Look at this like you look at capital projects. Most companies will commit cash to a capital

Worksheet 4.5   *Minimum* Return Rate

1. Benefit: Inventory $ _____ Carrying Cost
    (Worksheet 4.1—Line #8)
2. Benefit: Market $ _____
    (Worksheet 4.2—Line #10)
3. Benefit: Utilization $ _____
    (Worksheet 4.3—Line #5)
4. Total Benefit Potential $ _____
    (#1 + #2 + #3)
5. Gross Project Cost $ _____
    (Worksheet 4.4—Line #4)
6. Inventory Offset $ _____ 1-Time Reduction
    (Worksheet 4.1—Line #6)
7. Net Project Cost (#5 – #6) $ _____
8. Annual Return (#4/#7)·100   _____ %

project that returns 20%; after all, you can borrow the capital at 10%. *All companies* will do a project that returns 30%.

So, ... should you do this?

How Will We Know When We're Done?

- All business team members have read this first section.
- Estimates made of:

Ct	Lt
Vt	MCE
1st Pass Yield	Market Share %
Capacity Utilization	Bottleneck Location
On-time service %	

- Benefits worksheets completed and blessed by business team. (And a reasonable/attractive return is indicated.)
- Preliminary business team discussions have been conducted concerning

  Where a project should be located (Specific plant/product and/ or area)

  Probable Steering Team, Core Team, and Leader

When you've done this, and everyone is happy, please proceed to Section 2.

SECTION 2

Organization and Metrics

You tell me how you're going to measure me....
I'll tell you how I'm going to perform.

—Eli Goldratt

CHAPTER 5

The Process Industry and the "We're Different" Syndrome

This section begins the real work of implementing a Time strategy and will deal with organization, with metrics, and with how senior management resources and facilitates a Time strategy effort.

As we've said, this thought process, this improvement process, applies to any type of work process—a manufacturing process or a paperwork process. If you are considering a manufacturing process, these methods certainly apply. These ideas began in discrete parts, in fab and assembly, in screw-nut-bolt operations. So there is no question of application there; successful examples abound.

But there is reasonable doubt when you consider continuous operations or "process" operations. I want to begin this section with the assumption that you are from a process or continuous operation and that you have doubts. Your doubts are what I call the "We're Different" syndrome.

All of the comments in Box 5.1 may be true, but they miss the point. The manufacturing revolution in the 1980s that swept the auto industry, then the auto parts suppliers, and then all of discrete parts was a *flexibility* revolution. The JIT concept, the Toyota Production System, and the original ideas of Pull or Kanbans were all based on flexibility. The Toyota System, for example, grew from SMED[19] (Single Minute

61

Box 5.1 "We're Different"

- "We have massive equipment. It can't be rearranged into work cells."
- "Transitions are very difficult; they take a long time and generate much reject material. We can't consider small-lot production."
- "A feature of JIT/Toyota/Kanban systems is operator line stop. Our operations take hours or days to start up or shut down. We can't consider operator line stop."
- "Besides, we're continuous already!"

Exchange of Die) and was based on the ability to make small lots, or even lots of one unit.

The basic premise of JIT was concerned with two types of manufacturing costs: *scale* costs and *variety* costs (see Figure 5.1). As the company strives for higher volume, greater variety is required and that brings with it the increased costs associated with more transitions, more difficult quality, more complex inventory management, and so on. Those cost increases are offset by the advantage of spreading fixed costs—depreciation, taxes, administration, and labor (to some extent)—over a broader sales volume. In this model, the optimum point is where total costs are minimized.

The basic concept within flexible manufacturing is to drive down the flexibility costs, to accommodate higher variety without excessive costs. This comes by learning to make transitions easily and quickly without quality penalties. As you do that and pull the flexibility cost line down, two things happen: The minimum cost point comes *down* and also moves *out* (see Figure 5.2). This capability was a true revolution in manufacturing strategy. All the previous post–World War II strategies—low labor cost, economies of scale, focused factories—had two distinct weaknesses. They were *policy* strategies and they involved *trade-off* management.

The earlier strategies were policy strategies in that they did not incorporate any durable competitive advantage; they were simple man-

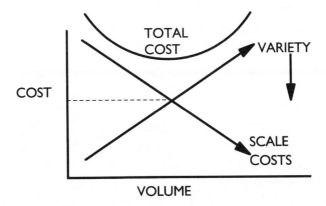

Figure 5.1 Scale and Variety Costs Define an Optimum

agement actions that offered temporary advantage but, once understood, were easily duplicable by all others. As such, when they were
introduced, they severely disrupted the playing field. But once the
competitors understood the strategy, all adopted the new approach,
and the environment stabilized as a standoff for all.

The other disadvantage of strategies that preceded JIT was tradeoff management. Trade-off management says that anything is possible
... *at a price* (see Box 5.2). JIT, or flexible manufacturing, was totally
different. It was able to offer price, quality, cost, and service improve-

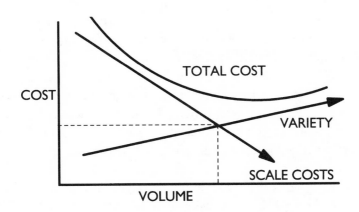

Figure 5.2 Reduced Variety Cost Impact

Box 5.2 Trade-Off Management

- "You want better quality? Fine, I'll just tighten quality specifi-cations. Of course, that means I'll reject more and costs will go up accordingly."
- "You want better customer service? Fine, I'll build a bigger, closer warehouse and increase inventory that I hold for you." (Never mind that the cost of that service *has* to be built into the next price quote.)
- "Want lower cost? Fine, but I can't give you all the product varieties we have been offering."

---

ments simultaneously. For that reason, flexibility was a true and durable competitive advantage because it was not easily duplicable by others; it was a skill or capability that acted as a shield against competition. It is that unique capability that was developed by discrete manufacturers that seems to be unachievable by process manufacturers and leads to the "We're different" belief.

But I would maintain that flexibility was not really the key. As discrete plants learned to make small lots, an artifact of small lots was that *time* was shrunk. If I make a long runs of each product in my portfolio, then I necessarily will have large amounts of inventory and long Cycle Time. As I learn to make quick changeovers and therefore to make small lots, a fallout is that inventory piles shrink and time disappears.

So there are some questions (shown in Box 5.3) that I think diffuse the issue. I would maintain that most of the gains came from *time elimination*. If I see a large pile of inventory, I know that Cycle Time is high (that is obvious from the basic formula; Ct = Inventory/Demand). But I also know that the pile represents nonvalue activities such as waiting, transporting, counting, probably some obsolescence and rework, and so on. If I extract time by making sure the pile is kept at a logical minimum, then I also extract waste.

Similarly, see Box 5.4. What we're describing here is a spiral of improvement that occurs. As we take waste activities out, stations become more closely connected. As they become connected, cause-and-

---

Box 5.3   The Questions That Diffuse "We're Different"

Where did the JIT improvement *really* come from?

- Did it come as a result of *flexibility?*
- Or did it come from the reduction of *time* in the process?

---

effect relations become more apparent. As we correct interrelated causes of waste, yet more waste is eliminated and the connection becomes stronger.

So I would maintain that time reduction was at least a very significant factor in the JIT revolution in the 1980s. What some of us have

---

Box 5.4   A Time Basic

If I am a supplier to you, and if I run faster than you can consume, then inventory will build up between us. As that happens, we become disconnected.

- If I make something that is *bad,* it will be a long time before you find it. (The pile is big.)
- When you find it, you don't care! (You have many others to choose from.)
- When you find it, I don't care! (I made that last Tuesday, and I am certainly not doing that now!)

The result is I go right on making bad stuff!

However, if I make something, hand it to you, and you throw it right back at me, we are connected. Cause/effect relationships are obvious, and I respond to what you (my customer) feed back to me.

Box 5.5   Why "We're Different" Isn't Valid

The basic strategy in this manual is all about attacking time. We are not necessarily talking about demanding flexibility or small lot production.

---

recognized is this: *You can go after time without necessarily going after flexibility.* In fact, as you will see later, you can sometimes get time out of an operation by being *more inflexible*.

Look again at the "We're Different" objections listed in Box 5.1. They all are true, *if your objective is flexibility*. None are true if your objective is time reduction (see Box 5.5).

Special Problems

I have continued to stress that the Time approach will work in any situation—manufacturing process or paperwork process, discrete or continuous environments. But application of these strategies will be primarily in manufacturing; process operations are a significant part of that environment, and they have distinctive features and problems. So I must define what I mean by the process industry. (It was defined briefly in Section 1, but a more detailed discussion is important to where we're going.)

The problem is that *there is no exact definition of the process industry.* That is, there is no real-world situation that is purely process; all operations are a mix. Continuous processes produce discrete finished packages (drum, bag, hopper car, etc.). Discrete operations have aspects of continuous as it deals in runs or batches of a specific part or product.

A much better distinction (as outlined in Section 1) is *diverging* and *converging*. Generally, traditional discrete operations take many parts and assemble them into one finished product, a car for example.

Box 5.6   A Process Industry Definition

A process operation is a diverging operation: Many end products are made from few raw materials; process equipment is general purpose and usually massive.

Process operations diverge, producing many different product variations through one process step (a coater, a paper machine, a reactor, an extruder, etc.). The definition of process industry presented in Box 5.6 incorporates the concept of divergence. See *Synchronous Manufacturing* by M. L. Srikanth for a complete discussion of divergence.

Divergence Problems

The distinguishing feature of divergence is that, at each production point, there are multiple production options (see Figure 5.3). In this example, if the emphasis is on production volume, Intermediate B will be converted into whatever will optimize immediate performance. If E is the best/easiest/optimum choice, that is what will be done. If resources (people, equipment, or, most important, inventory) are consumed to produce Product E, and then we later find that the product really needed was G, those resources are not recoverable; they have been *irreversibly* committed.

Moreover, let's assume we are dealing with the *bottleneck* step in the operation (all operations have one definitive bottleneck step, the one point where capacity is most highly utilized). If you make a wrong decision on committal of resources through the bottleneck step, you have wasted capacity of *the entire operation or process*. (Capacity of the entire operation is defined by the capacity of the bottleneck.)

This is *the* fundamental challenge in managing diverging operations—the conflict between the push for production and the problem

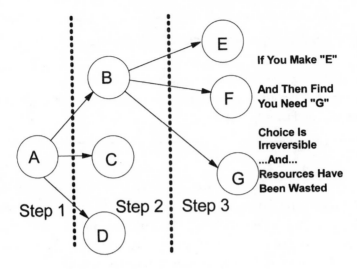

Figure 5.3 Divergence Is a Problem of Choice

Box 5.7 Characteristics of Diverging Operations

- High finished product inventory
- Inability to meet customer orders
- Marketing dissatisfaction with manufacturing service
- Manufacturing dissatisfaction with market "churn" and poor forecasts
- Manufacturing desire for longer Lead Time

Box 5.8 BAU Divergence Strategies

- Exotic and computerized forecasting methods
- Sophisticated MRP scheduling systems
- Centralized inventory and distribution management
- Long production cycles to isolate manufacturing from market variations
- Long lead times to protect manufacturing
- Better service through higher inventory

**Box 5.9   New Management Paradigms
for Managing Process
(Diverging) Operations**

- Resist committing resources until demand is known.
- Hold inventory *early* in the process. Inventory loses utility as it becomes more personalized.
- Insert customer orders as *early* in the manufacturing supply chain as possible.
- Work to extract time from the process or operation. The *only* way to improve forecast accuracy is to reduce Cycle Time so that you don't have to reach out as far with your forecast.
- Manage the trade-off between customer Lead Time, On-Time delivery performance, and required inventory. (Two of these three parameters can be set by management policy, but the third must float to whatever is dictated by current operating capability.)

---

of committing resources before the end need is known. This paradox results in the characteristic problems within a process or diverging operation shown in Box 5.7.

Traditional management tries to solve the divergence problem with traditional strategies (see Box 5.8). Those of us who have been there know that these strategies don't work; they actually encourage production that isn't needed. Excess production means longer Cycle Times through the plant, which means that forecasts are less accurate, which means more just-in-case inventory, and so on. Resolution of these problems requires some new paradigms for managing (see Box 5.9). The methods and techniques for managing in this manner are tied up in Pull Scheduling systems. We'll go into detail concerning Pull in Section 4.

CHAPTER 6

Organizing for a Time Implementation

The entire structure for conducting/managing a Time project is shown in Figure 6.1.

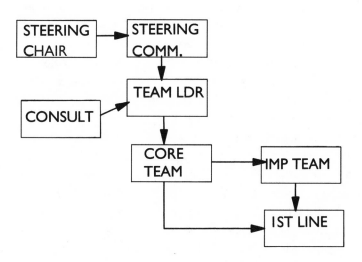

Figure 6.1 Organizing for Time

The Steering Team

As we have stressed previously, a Time effort must be business related. It *cannot* be a manufacturing effort, driven for manufacturing's benefit. An example is shown in Box 6.1. The moral of the example is, Time efforts must be clearly driven by business issues.

Ensuring that efforts are business driven and objectives are clear to all is the role of the Steering Team. The importance of the Steering Team is illustrated by another example, presented in Box 6.2.

The functions of the Steering Team are shown in Box 6.3.

Box 6.1   Time Strategy: A Manufacturing Initiative? An Example

---

Our initial Du Pont experiments were under the sponsorship of the Manufacturing Committee. As such, the business viewed us as an effort to benefit manufacturing; they didn't trust our motive.

Our first effort was in X-ray film production. In short order, we were able to take Cycle Time in the plant from 53 days to 12 days, while the customer Lead Time was 30 days. We had created a situation where we were able to move from an environment of producing to inventory by means of forecasts to an environment of producing to firm customer order, *and* we were in position to either offer shorter lead times or cut internal inventories.

Given that improvement within the plant, you would also expect a collapse in the distribution system's inventory: If the plant is much more responsive, you should not need as much just-in-case inventory in the field.

But marketing/sales did not trust our motives, did not understand our accomplishments, and feared that we would benefit ourselves. As a protective measure, they actually *built* distribution inventories. The business as a larger whole got no benefit from the internal plant gains (until we went through extensive explanations and a long and careful demonstration period).

Box 6.2 A Steering Team Disconnection: Another Example

I recently did extensive work with a polyethylene resin producer. One of the core opportunities was around inventory reduction by a change in scheduling strategies. Because of severe limits on intermediate inventory, the company was often unable, in the moment, to make the specific final product needed. So it made what it could! As a result, the firm had huge inventories of everything but what it currently needed.

We did a good job of getting plant management understanding and support. With that, we did a great job of developing scheduling strategies that built internal intermediate inventories that then allowed ability to produce final product on demand and offered dramatic reductions in finished product inventories.

Our problem was that the effort was plant-internal, and scheduling had always been done by corporate central. The Steering Team failed to make a good connection with them, their security was threatened by our proposals, and we did not have business level understanding and support.

The result was that we were delayed almost a year in achieving a multimillion dollar business gain, because we had not properly done the Steering Team work.

Box 6.3 Functions of the Steering Team

- Set performance metrics. What do we expect to influence?
- Provide initial resources. Staff the Core Team.
- Receive recommendations from the Core Team.
- The Core Team Sets priorities and selects action.
- Resolve conflicts between functional groups.
- Provide funding/resources for action items.
- Measure success against objectives.

The makeup of the Steering Team should have all aspects of the business team represented (see Box 6.4).

Selection of the specific Steering Team members needs to meet at least two criteria:

1. Members need to be capable of reflecting high-level business needs and objectives.
2. The Steering Team needs to be accessible to the Core Team. At the very least, their regular meetings need to be held at the plant (video or phone conference is not acceptable. Between meetings, if surprises occur, the Core Team Leader needs to have easy access to the Steering Team chairman to discuss the problem.

The general function of the Steering Team can be depicted in flow-chart format: The function is to provide direction, receive recommendations, advise on priorities and practicalities, and provide implementation resources (see Figure 6.2). In this depiction, the opportunities are provided and programs actually implemented by the Core Team under the authority, strategic direction, and with resources provided by the Steering Team.

The Steering Team typically meets about twice per month. Initially, these meetings are to consider the direction and the health of the business, to set performance metrics based on critical success factors for the business, to verify that they will endorse and support a Time effort, and to set up the Time organization. As such, these are working meet-

---

Box 6.4   Steering Team Membership

- Business manager. (Person with profit responsibility)
- Manufacturing. (Owner of plant[s])
- Sales/marketing. (May be separate functions)
- Research/development.
- Scheduling.
- Distribution. (Inventory/warehousing)

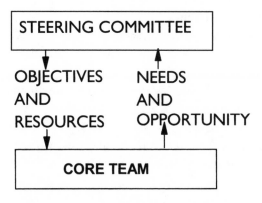

Figure 6.2 The Steering/Core Interface

ings. They may extend to several hours or a full day per meeting, and the meetings have specific work product objectives.

Once the organization is in place and the Core Team begins to function, the Steering Team is not a working committee, it is an oversight and approval committee. Meetings are concise—one to two hours on an agenda set by the Core Team Leader. The hard detail work takes place in the Core Team meetings.

Often, the Steering Team can be a revision or an expansion of an existing team. The plant management staff usually contains most of the functions that are needed, with the exception of sales/marketing and sometimes the central scheduling/distribution/warehousing person. It is sometimes practical for the Steering Team to meet as an extension of their regular meeting; they take off their regular hats, put on their Steering Team hats, and conduct their business. But it is important that the Time portion of the meeting be *distinct and separate*. It is also *sometimes* reasonable that the people in remote functions attend by means of conference call (assuming all paperwork has been faxed to them before the meeting). On critical issues, however, attendance in person is usually important. It is simply too easy for remote members to defer their responsibility, become disconnected, and later become an un-understanding resistance.

Once the Steering Team is formed, the members have five distinct tasks, *before* the Core Team can begin to function:

1. Staff the Core Team.
2. Set boundaries for the project.
3. Develop a rollout or expansion plan for this effort.
4. Set performance metrics.
5. Provide facilities and resources for the Core Team.

These tasks flow in a logical and necessary order, and each is vital to the success of the overall effort. These are discussed in detail in Chapters 7 and 8 of this section.

Staffing and Supporting the Core Team

THE CORE TEAM LEADER

Obviously, this is a critical position. The Steering Team selects the Team Leader, and the Leader participates with the Steering Team in fleshing out the Time team. Characteristics of the Leader are shown in Box 6.5, and a discussion of who you may not want to choose as the Leader follows in Box 6.6.

The Team Leader is usually a respected plant technical engineer or a manufacturing area supervisor. See the "Resourcing the Team" section in this chapter and "The Consultant" section in Chapter 8 for additional considerations concerning this Leader.

THE CORE TEAM MEMBERS

The Core Team does the detailed analytical and planning work and consists of representatives from all affected areas and includes some people with special skills. Typical teams will consist of representatives from:

Box 6.5   Core Team Leader Characteristics

- **Visibility.** The leader should be well known and respected on the floor.
- **Communication Skills.** The Leader should be equally comfortable working at the level of the business team and on the shop floor. He or she should have good oral and written communications skills and be a skillful presenter.
- **Team Skills.** The Leader should be capable of facilitating accomplishments of the team, as opposed to promoting personal recognition.
- **Project Management Skills.** The Leader should be able to formulate programs, develop time lines, assign or create responsibility, adjust to changes or developments, and maintain accountability.
- **No Baggage.** The Leader should be open to change; he or she should have no personal stake in the current operation.

- Each involved manufacturing area.
- Maintenance (if maintenance effectiveness is likely to be an issue).
- Scheduling: local plant scheduling and (perhaps) centralized inventory/distribution/warehousing/scheduling group.

Box 6.6   Who You May Not Want

Every widget plant has a "Mr. Widget," someone who has put many years into literally inventing the current plant. Some Steering Teams feel they are making the extreme commitment by selecting Mr. Widget as the Team Leader. The problem is that Widget has put so much effort into creating the current state that he can't begin to conceive of anything different; any suggestion of change is taken as a personal affront. The Leader should have no personal baggage about the current situation.

- QC lab. Sometimes, the quality lab turns out to be the bottleneck step for the manufacturing operation. If material in the shop is sitting, waiting on lab quality results, that adds to Cycle Time and to waste.
- Technical. This need not be someone with detailed technical knowledge of this manufacturing process. This person brings the analytical and data management skills that the team will require.
- Information Systems (IS). Initially, this person is needed to dig in Info Systems to get the data the team needs. It is common that accessing the production, inventory, capacity, demand, waste/yield/recovery, and cost data needed by the team to do their analysis, is not easy. This person is called upon to utilize the system to get or to estimate the information needed. Later, this person will advise IS on changing needs for current or future information systems as a result of items implemented by the Core Team. (This process deals in simple, visual management tools that may alter or negate computerized systems.)
- A model builder. One possible part of the Core Team work may be to build a simulation model of the operation to aid understanding of a difficult or complex operation and/or to test controversial or expensive changes on a PC before committing to action on the real floor. If you think modeling might be valuable, identify the person and then let the Core Team make the final decision. The candidate does not need sophisticated prior programming skills. The person does need a logical/analytical bent and needs to be a detail bulldog. Modeling is discussed in more detail in Section 3.

When we began to staff Core Teams within Du Pont, we approached staffing with our usual bias toward degreed technical people. Our teams were largely or completely composed of salaried and/or management personnel. As we progressed, we learned the value of involving shop floor hourly people. Eventually, most manufacturing and maintenance reps were wage (hourly) roll, and local scheduling people also frequently came from the hourly force. We learned that hourly people often knew more about what made up the real world. (Management knew what it said in the manuals and technical bulletins, but that often only had a loose connection with what went on out on the floor.)

If you want to implement on the shop floor, you are better off having the shop floor design that implementation. *Ownership* is the offspring of *involvement*.

Resourcing the Team: Full-Time or Part-Time?

What I have described above is a team that might range in size from four to eight people. The task that they are undertaking can require six to nine months to accomplish. In today's environment, it is no easy matter to find that number of capable people available for full-time assignment. No one has people just waiting around for something to do.

I'll offer several options or considerations.

- Full- or Part-Time. The usual first answer to the problem of re-sourcing teams is to want to do this part-time in addition to team members' regular assignments. Although mentioned earlier, I want to be perfectly clear on this issue: Part-time assignments are a *huge* mistake.

  The problem with part-time teams is twofold:

  1. Part-time members will always make sure that their own personal world is optimized before they concern themselves with the optimization of the team. If I believe my performance appraisal and rating will primarily be influenced by my regular job accomplishments, I will be sure to devote all needed at-

> Part-time teams will take four times as long and will achieve half the benefits of a full-time team!

tention to that—first. If I am subject to night/weekend work, unwanted or uncompensated overtime, or night/weekend phone calls, I'll do what is necessary to resolve those problems—first.

2. With part-time teams, the environment changes faster than the team can analyze and characterize that environment. I once visited a plant that had chartered a part-time team that had been looking at implementing Pull Scheduling by means of two-hour meetings every Wednesday. They had been meeting for a full year and did not yet have a plan in place! I very recently worked with a plant that had had a pseudo Core Team in place for about a year without an end in sight, who then completed their work in two months once they committed three full-time people.

- Regular vs. Extended Team members. Some organizations recognize that *some portion* of the team can be effectively staffed by part-time members while the team activities progress on a full-time basis. The regular team works full-time and calls on the extended team as their special knowledge is needed. Lab, maintenance, associated production areas, SQC or SPC teams, IS, and so on are possible candidates for extended team membership.

- Multiple teams. If you will have multiple projects—either multiple products on the same site, multiple areas done singly on the same plant, or multiple plants—you have the opportunity to share resources. In Du Pont, we were dealing with more than 100 sites worldwide and many of those sites had multiple products. The usual approach was to group plants together in sets of four to six, and each plant contributed a person to a team that did the work at the first plant. Not only did that provide resources for that first plant, the individuals each gained the knowledge to return to their plant as an informed and effective leader for their own plant team. The only problem with this approach was, once the sister plants saw the surprising benefits the parent plant got, every other plant in the group wanted to be resourced immediately.

- Finally, can you afford not to do this and do it well? Every plant is different, but over the course of many implementations, some typical benefits emerge. It is not unusual to see benefits such as those

---

Box 6.7   Typical Benefits or Results (1st Year)

Inventory:	40% Reductions
Capacity:	20% Increase
Cycle Time:	50% Reduction
Yields:	5% to 15% Increase in Final Yield
Service:	Sharply reduced Lead Time
	-or-
	Improved On-Time delivery
Market Share:	Increased share based on better partnerships with key customers
Productivity:	Better utility of management and technical people through reassignment from fire fighting to improvement

---

listed in Box 6.7. Based on that magnitude of improvement, I have never seen a team that didn't deliver benefits in their first year at least equal to their total cost. Typically, benefits far exceed first-year costs and have ranged up to 10 to 30 times the company's project costs (see Box 6.8). When you offset project cost with the cash-flow benefit of inventory reductions, net out-of-pocket cost may well be zero!

Box 6.8   The Fundamental Resourcing Question

Do you have any other project or program competing for assignments that offer 100% to 3000% return on investment?

CHAPTER 7

Performance Metrics

The single most critical task of the Steering Team is to set performance metrics. Enough has already been said about metrics and behavior; they are synonymous.

Section 1 also listed typical BAU metrics, shown in Box 7.1. As previously discussed, these metrics act to encourage production, even if that production is not immediately needed. "Make whatever you can. We'll sell it eventually." And, as also shown, excess production adds to Cycle Time and causes disconnection between stations.

In contrast, Box 7.2 lists some metrics that are more consistent with a Time approach. So one thing the Steering Team will want to do is examine any current metrics and challenge any that may be inconsistent with Time principles. *This is not a trivial task!* To challenge current metrics is a very difficult assignment because, to give up a closely held metric, you must give up current management paradigms.

Box 7.1 Traditional (BAU) Metrics

- Cost per unit of production
- Labor per unit of production (lower is better)
- Production total per accounting period (higher is better)
- Fixed cost per unit of production
- Capacity utilization (higher is better)
- Idle time (idle is bad)
- Inventory (inventory as an *asset*)
- Capacity impact of transitions, or campaign length (long runs maximize capacity and protect manufacturing from sales demand variations)
- Capacity of a production unit or line (bigger, wider, more powerful is better)

Box 7.2 Time Metrics

- Cycle Time (Inventory/Demand)
- Capability (Cp)
- 1st Pass Yield
- Customer Service
  —Order Lead Time
  —On-Time Delivery
- Market Share
- Capacity Utilization
- New Product Development
- Financials
  —Earnings
  —Margin
  —Return on Equity
  —Contribution to Shareholder Value

How Many Metrics?

I have seen businesses with more than 40 performance metrics. One of the very basic ideas of Time, however, is *focus,* the selection of only a few very fat rabbits. How is it possible to focus when one is dealing with 40 metrics? There is no hard and fast rule, but the structure we're going to use will limit us to eight high-level strategies plus supporting tactics.

Revisiting Current Metrics

The first step for the Steering Team—before staffing the Core Team, providing facilities, and so on—is to test, challenge, and revise performance metrics. How do you know *how* to achieve your objectives until you are clear as to *what* those objectives are?

Here the specific test for the Steering Team is to establish what current metrics really are. Do this for at least three levels in the organization: strategic, management, and operational. Do this by having the business management itemize the critical success factors and key strategies for the business. Keep the list to about a half-dozen key items. Then, at the operational and at the management levels ask, "How is your performance measured?" You'll probably get a lot of blank stares in response to that question. Track the answers for consistency and for connection with the key strategies. This is only a measure of how you are currently doing in communicating objectives through your organization and linking those objectives to individual performance evaluations. We will later test and revise our strategies, and if we find that we have not been doing a good job of communicating standards in the past, we'll want to work doubly hard on the new or revised metrics.

In my own work, when I ask the "How are you measured?" question, I find a lot of disconnection. The best single situation I've seen involved a small institutional (school and hospital) furniture company. The corporate staff had decided that their main objective was to grow market share and that their tactic for doing that was to become the most reliable and most responsive supplier. On-time performance became their key strategy. What I saw when I tested their organization was the following:

- A large sign at the main gate that displayed two items: safety performance yesterday and to date, and on-time performance percentage for the preceding day.
- If there had been a delayed order the previous day, everyone knew the details.
- Everyone knew the way they could influence on-time performance and had a personal metric that tied back to on-time performance so that they could measure their own contribution to the company strategy.

Resetting Metrics: Identifying the Corners

A first issue in setting metrics is to define and understand the playing field: the environment that you're living in and the masters that you serve. To be sure that you have a balanced approach and are strong throughout your environment, it helps to name the four corners of that field (see Figure 7.1).

The idea of a playing field was suggested by Kaplan and Norton's work titled *The Balanced Scorecard* (Harvard Business Press, 1996). They specify the four aspects of their scorecard. They are:

1. *Customer Perspective.* What does the customer value; what does he or she need to succeed? How can we establish partnerships and share the supply chain in a mutually beneficial way?
2. *Internal Perspective.* What must we excel at? To satisfy all our stakeholders, what internal skills and core competencies are needed?

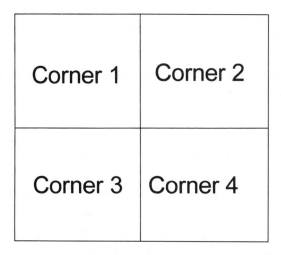

Figure 7.1   Our Playing Field or Environment

3. *Innovation.* The first two parameters deal primarily with the current state, what the perspective is today. Innovation deals with how our environment is evolving and what skills will be needed in the future. Candidate considerations include all aspects of understanding your future: changes in the perspectives of customers, competitors, employees, community, government influence, and emerging technologies. All these can or will influence how you will be required to innovate and the new internal skills that will be required.
4. *Financial Perspective.* The measures here are generally obvious: profit margin, return on investment/equity, earnings per share, and ultimately stock price.

You won't go wrong at all if you use these definitions. But, as one individual, I do have some questions or reservations. My concern with this approach is that it seems overly rigid, and that Internal Perspective seems redundant to Customer and Financial Perspectives. The core competencies we must have are determined by what we must deliver to the market and to the stockholder. Conversely, we shed or outsource tasks that we don't do well in order to meet financial goals. Therefore, Internal Perspective would seem to be nested under the higher-level

---

Box 7.3   A Suggested Four Corners

- The Customer or the Marketplace
- The Stockholder
- The Community
- The Future (Innovation)

---

concern for those prime masters, customer and stockholder. (See the later discussion distinguishing between "strategy" and "tactics.")

Conversely, it seems to me that Norton and Kaplan don't give enough weight to social/community responsibilities—employee, community, environmental concerns. Therefore, my personal modification to the Balanced Scorecard is to identify the four corners of *my* environment as in Box 7.3. What is important, I feel, is to think about and carefully identify your own particular four corners. You'll want to be sure that your four selections *truly* are far apart and define the extremes of the playing field. As we've just seen, it's easy to name corners that are really redundant alternative expressions.

A partial list of "candidate" corners would include:

- The Market or Customer
- The Stockholder
- The Employee
- The Environment
- The Future (Growth and Learning)
- The Community
- Internal Skills

There are two ways that you might conduct the corner-identifying session:

1. Multivoting
   - List suggestions from the group.
   - Eliminate any that are restatements of the same objective.

- From your local stationery store, give everyone four stick-on dots. The rules are that they may stick those dots to objectives however they choose: four dots on one objective, one dot each on four objectives, and so on.
- Test the top four to be sure you don't have redundant objectives. Condense, restate, and test the new top four.
- Continue until you have four distinct corners.

2. Strategy Grouping

In Section 3 we will discuss the Seven Management Tools: simple paper-and-pencil tools for organizing and planning management programs and initiatives. One of those is the Affinity Diagram. In brief, execution of an Affinity Diagram is done by posting a group of ideas, each on a 3-by-5-inch card or Post-it, onto a wall or display board. Those are then grouped into logical and related subgroups. Each grouping is given a summary title card. If that activity has not reduced the ideas to a manageable number of summary groups, the grouping activity is done again with the summary cards. Eventually, the beginning array is reduced to a few number of core or key concepts. Affinity Diagrams can be used to define corners:

- Ask people to post all the key strategies, thrusts, programs, and so on that they see as being critical to the health of the company. Be sure to include social responsibilities as well as financial.
- Conduct the grouping and summarizing process, putting together all cards that seem to address the same concern.
- Cease when you have reduced the array to four fundamental concerns. You've named the four corners!

Strategies in the Corners

Once we've defined the four corners, we're ready to define strategies and tactics for each. First, we need to be precise as to what we mean by those two terms, and look at how they "nest" together.

Strategic Metrics: In my definition, strategic metrics determine direction for the organization. They define what are critical success factors for the organization—*what* the organization must achieve, *where* it must go.

Tactical Metrics: These describe *how* the objective is to be achieved. They define specific action to be taken. Tactical metrics determine or dictate shop floor action.

Nested Metrics: The idea of *nested* metrics is related to the concept of strategic versus tactical metrics. Some performance metrics are contained within broader or higher-level metrics. For example, yield is contained within cost, as the objective of reduced cost can be obtained by improving yield. Machine uptime is nested within customer service which in turn is nested within market share. A company may decide that a critical success factor is gaining increased market share and that improved customer service is the prime way to attack share. In turn, improved machine uptime may be the prime way to improve service.

(Note that the reference is to "metrics." This implies *measurable*. We don't want strategies or tactics that are subjective. Further, we want measurements that are simple, straightforward, and unquestionable. If you need to dig in the bowels of your computer system to generate the metric, no one will understand it, and no one will trust the result.)

One of my main concerns in making this distinction is that business teams or senior management spends a lot of time on *tactics* and not nearly enough time on *strategy*. At any level, and certainly at the senior level, it is critical that clear strategy be determined and then communicated to the supporting level(s). That supporting level then determines the best tactics for achieving the strategy. Thus, I believe that *no one* but senior management can determine strategy. The working level depends on clear management strategy. But senior management is not competent to determine tactics, because they are not intimate to the floor.

A specific example will illustrate my point. A Du Pont Director of Manufacturing for one of our major departments declared that all parts of all plants would conduct Total Productive Maintenance (TPM) pro-

> The Charge of the Light Brigade was ordered by an officer who had not seen the territory.

grams. Now, I am a proponent of TPM, and it may well be that TPM would be beneficial for many areas—perhaps for most areas—but I can guarantee that it was not *the best* focus item for *all* areas *at that specific time*. Those areas that did not need TPM had two choices: either dutifully do TPM to no benefit or do two programs (TPM and whatever they *did* need to do) only partially well. This is a perfect example of the strategic level of the organization dictating tactics at the shop floor.

There is another reason for being sure to set strategic metrics and avoiding dictating tactical metrics. Tactical metrics are measured or reportable by the level that executes the tactic. Example: Uptime is a shop floor tactic, and the measuring/reporting of uptime is by the shop floor. If you dictate to me that my performance is to be measured by a particular tactic, I'm going to be sure that I report good performance to you.

When at Du Pont, I did work for a product that had six producing plants in four different countries around the world. The director of that global operation dictated that 1st Pass Yield would be the prime metric. Would it surprise you that all plants reported performance within 2% of each other, all in the low 90s? Further, would it surprise you that when we did a detailed analysis, we found that actual performance was very different plant-to-plant, ranging from the 60% to the 80% range? Finally, would it surprise you that much of that difference was due to real differences in products and technologies between plants? What had happened was that each plant determined its own ground rules about how Yield was reported, so that its reported number was competitive with others. No one recognized that the rules were different, in order to ensure that the numbers were not different. The point is, dictated tactical metrics from Mecca only ensured that there would be no distinctions or impact of those metrics.

In contrast, if you tell me your strategy, and I tell you what my tactic in support of that strategy will be, I'm going to make sure that I can show improvement in my tactical area. I'll confess to you how bad things really are now, and then I'll work hard to show improvement. And since you measure the strategy, you should be able to see improvement as a result of my tactical efforts. For example, if you decide that a critical business strategy is market share by better customer service, and I decide my tactic for better service is reducing transition time, I should be able to show improvement in transitions, you should see results of that in better service, and if your analysis of the market is correct, share gains should result.

Further, one level's tactics appear as the strategy for or to the supporting level in the organization. The CEO defines strategic direction for the company. Divisional VPs develop tactics to deliver against that strategy. Those tactics become the strategic direction for the division and are communicated to the group managers, who develop their tactics to support the direction of the division. Those group tactics are expressed to the plant sites as their strategic direction, for which the plants develop their supporting tactics. And so on, straight to the first-line supervisor, who attempts to deliver against the area supervisor's objectives by instituting tactics and metrics for his or her team. In this way, strategy and tactics extend in an unbroken, logical, and integrated chain from the CEO to the shop floor.

We'll begin to build that chain by defining the high-level strategies in each corner. The method is simple; the result is critical. For each individual corner:

1. Brainstorm all possible strategies. (Remember the brainstorming rule: At this point, all ideas are good ideas.)
2. Strike off or combine any duplications.
3. Test each remaining item to see if it truly is a high-level strategy. The test is to ask, "Why would we do this?" If there is a higher objective—if the answer is "so that we can achieve X"—then X is the higher strategy and should replace the original strategy statement. If there is no "so that," that is, if the reason is self-evident, then you have a *true* strategy.
4. Conduct a multivote process. (Rule of thumb: Give each person a number of "dots" equal to one-third of the number of ideas on the list.)

5. There will be a sharp drop-off point somewhere in the resultant ranking. Strike every one below that cutoff point.
6. Conduct the multivote again, giving each participant only two votes.
7. Take *only* the top two strategies! (The reason for the limit is that we are going to develop supporting tactics and each strategy may require multiple tactics. If we don't impose this limit, we could end with too many directives to the operating levels.)

Some Suggested Strategic Metrics

CUSTOMER/MARKET

What I would identify as a critical strategy under Customer goes right back to the basics of Cycle Time. Given that the basic Cycle Time formula is Inventory divided by Demand, it follows that, if you are trying to reduce Cycle Time, then you are interested in both reducing inventory *and increasing demand*. Too often, managers become fixated on inventory, while assuming that volume or market share is a given.

Goldratt (*The Goal*) has a lot to say on the subject of demand. His basic principle is that every process has a bottleneck, a single and definitive bottleneck. If you manage and optimize the bottleneck, you have optimized the entire system. He is so adamant that he maintains that there is only one metric: the utilization of the bottleneck.

In terms of managing and increasing market share, there are really only two cases: either you are sold out or you are not. If you are sold out (and restricting sales accordingly), then your particular bottleneck is at capacity and acts to limit additional sales. However, in almost every case in my experience, when a team rigorously focuses on the bottleneck, they can find ways to extract additional capacity (better uptime, faster transitions, better downstream yield, more efficient schedules, etc.) When you can find that extra increment of capacity, you have found incremental earnings, revenue that comes only at the cost of providing additional materials (all the other components of cost are already paid). That is a *very* powerful position. When I encounter a client who says that he's sold out, I know that we're going to have a lot of fun together.

The other alternative is that you're not sold out. In that case, something is limiting your access to the market. That "something" must be either price, quality design, quality conformance to design, customer service, or your assumptions about the scope of your market. And all those have causes that reside within the plant. So whether or not you are sold out, increasing demand is completely within plant control.

Again quoting Goldratt, cost/profit analysis can be reduced to looking at three factors: sales revenue, cost of converting inventory into product, and capital invested in inventory and equipment to make that conversion. There are limitations on improving cost and investments (you can't reduce beyond zero) while increases in revenue are *unlimited*. (Remember, Goldratt says markets are limited only by your definition.)

This (finally) brings me to a suggested metric for this corner: *market share growth*.

MARKET SHARE GROWTH

If you are gaining market share, then you are enjoying increased incremental earnings and have those earnings to reinvest in your business. And you've done that at the expense of your competition: What you have gained, they have lost. This is so powerful a position that some experts maintain that this is *the key* metric.

Two recent quotes in *Fortune* magazine would indicate that this view is about to become a new wave:

Driving for growth is where companies should really get their reward in heaven.

George Fisher, CEO, Kodak
(formerly CEO, Motorola)

You've got to have growth to live. The idea that you can cost-reduce to prosperity has proven to be absolutely incorrect.

Larry Bossidy, CEO, Allied Signal

Bossidy's views are especially telling. Allied Signal stock value has increased 400% during his term. In the *Fortune* article, he maintains that no market is ever fully penetrated, that people are limited only by their own prejudices and lack of imagination.

STOCKHOLDER OR FINANCIAL

A suggestion for the strategic metric in this segment would be Contribution to Shareholder Value. Recently, Du Pont has enjoyed strong recognition from the financial community (share price up approximately 40% in 1996), and they are driving this metric hard. The formula is:

Shareholder Value = ATOI − (Cost of Money) · (Total Capital)

Where:

ATOI = After Tax Operating Income
Cost of Money = Borrowing/Interest Rate
Total Capital = All inventory and capital equipment

In that formula, ideally, Cost of Money is set at 12%, inventory is at market value (not at cost), and equipment is valued at selling price it would attract (not depreciated value and not at replacement cost). This has become Du Pont's prime measure of the health of each business segment; a positive contribution is the requirement to stay in the portfolio. And once faced with that requirement, it has been surprising how many businesses have been able to pull themselves above the line. Few businesses have been shed under this criteria.

As a cycle time purist, you can see why this metric would appeal to me. It forces one to get the most out of one's inventory and to use capital equipment to the fullest.

EMPLOYEE OR COMMUNITY

One critical aspect of this corner is that enduring success is increasingly tied to the "intellectual capital"[20] deployed by the company to create value. Retaining and growing that capital requires that the people who bring that capital, those who have critical knowledge not available to the employer, have a true sense of community, of belonging, of *owning* the business. For that reason, the growth of the information age has spawned growth in employee ownership of the corporation. Today, Microsoft ownership is equally split between those who invested financial capital and those who invested intellectual capital—the founders and employees. So this corner might well carry a strategy of growing employee ownership in the venture through stock-option plans.

WHAT ABOUT CYCLE TIME?

Should Ct appear as a strategic metric in one of the corners? Probably not. On its own it doesn't pass the "so what?" test for a strategic metric. When you ask the "Why?" question, you'll find that you are pursuing time to achieve a higher objective: service, inventory efficiency, greater markets, lower cost, and so on. But Cycle Time certainly should be a key tactic under one or more corner strategies. That leads us to the next task.

Building the Supporting Tactics

The strategies we've developed will be very effective in defining the direction of the business, but they won't be very meaningful to the shop floor. If you declare Return on Shareholder Equity to be a prime strategy in the Stockholder corner, the floor person won't have a clue as to how to respond.

The process of translating high-level strategies into meaningful tactics that the floor can respond to is referred to as building a *Tactics*

Tree. Building a tree uses another of the Seven Management Tools, a Program Planning Chart.

A Program Planning Chart begins with an objective that is not possible today. The question asked is "What would I have to have in place to make that objective possible?" When that question is answered, and there may be more than one item required, the next question is "Are those items possible today?" If not, you ask the "What would I have to have in place?" question again. You follow that sequence until you reach items that *are* possible today. Figure 7.2 shows what the resulting chart looks like. As noted, if you look at Figure 7.2 from left to right, the diagram answers how you are going to accomplish the objective. If you look from right to left, the chart shows why you are doing each item.

After defining the playing field and setting a limit of two strategies for each corner, the Steering Team can use the concepts of nested metrics and the Planning Chart to build a Tactics Tree that bridges to the shop floor. The key in building the tree is to go far enough so that the right-hand side identifies tactics that are very understandable and within the control of the floor, while stopping short of dictating specific action to the floor. For purposes of ownership, the floor needs to select the action that will best achieve an objective set out by management. An objective of better/faster on-time delivery is a meaningful

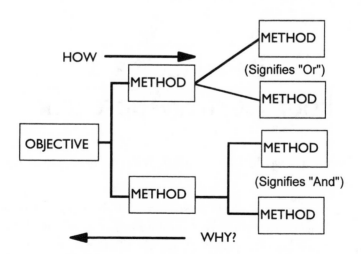

Figure 7.2 A Planning Chart or Tactics Tree

Box 7.4   Candidate Tactics

- Capability Index (Cp)
- Manufacturing Cycle Efficiency (Vt/Ct)
- 1st Pass Yield
- On-Time Delivery
- Capacity Utilization (Remember: There is an optimum that is less than 100%)
- Bottleneck Efficiency
- New Product Development Ct

---

objective, and many alternative things might be done to achieve that end. Improved machine uptime is a specific activity and, as an objective, leaves no room for creativity and initiative.

A further goal would be to build the tree with an eye to minimizing the objectives set out for the floor. That's why we limited the corner strategies to a maximum of two. One would hope the Tactics Tree for each corner would expand into no more than four tactics each.

Beyond Ct, other tactics that might appear somewhere in your tree are listed in Box 7.4.

Benefits of a Four Corner Approach

There are at least two disciplines that are imposed by Kaplan and Norton's basic concept:

1. Limited metrics and a focused perspective. A primary benefit of this approach is that it tends to minimize information overload by limiting the number of metrics imposed. My experience is that companies almost never suffer from too few metrics; they are usually drown-

ing in metrics and performance data. Remember the Du Pont example of the department with 40 performance measures. You can't focus if you don't have focused metrics.

Kaplan and Norton in their description of the balanced scorecard refer to the proliferation of metrics as the "kill another tree" problem. This approach forces focus on the few metrics that are truly important.

2. Second, this approach guards against suboptimization or local optimization within one of the four corners. It will be self-evident that strengths must be balanced over all corners. If one area is weak, eventually that will cause weakness in the others. If one area of performance is given priority at the expense of another, the results will make that obvious.

However, there is a concern or qualifier: the potential for a short-term and restrictive focus on this quarter's earnings and the impact on stock price. Is the company doing things to hype the stock price at the expense of the long-term health of the company? Certainly that happens, but with the balanced scorecard approach that should be obvious. If financials are improving without corresponding gain in the other corners (customer, internal skills, or innovation), then the long-term perspective is bleak.

The converse is, Will we make improvement in performance and not see a financial reward? The usual reason for this is that we fail to follow through and capitalize on an improvement. Quality and Cycle Time improvement can create incremental added capacity. If management does not either put that capacity to work by increased sales or get rid of it by reduced expenses, bottom line improvement will not result. If yields are increased, nonvalue inspection and rework activities fall away. If that productivity gain is not used to either reduce headcount or (better yet) to free people for more beneficial improvement work, then financials will not benefit. The classic example is improving capacity at other than the bottleneck process step. If you do not improve bottleneck capacity, you do not get more out the other end and you do not get financial reward. So, in the end, if gaining in internal performance is not gaining in financials, you must reexamine your Tactics Tree to be sure that you are capitalizing on that improvement and that there really is a connection direct to the bottom line. Not all strategies are profitable strategies.

CHAPTER 8

Other Organizational Tasks

Setting Boundaries for the Effort

With metrics and objectives defined, the next task is to consider guidelines for boundaries, or limits, on the project. These boundaries need to be set before the makeup of the Core Team can be set; if you don't know what is included, you don't know what functions need to be represented on the Core Team. These are only guidelines, because the first task for the Core Team will be to revisit this question. The question is twofold: What is *outside* the project, and what is *inside?*

I'm going to organize this section in the form of several questions the Steering Team needs to ask and answer. They are:

1. How far forward and backward in the supply chain does this project reach? The entire supply chain can extend all the way from the forecast that we might get an order through to receipt of payment for product delivered. It includes procurement of raw materials, processing

through the plant, warehousing of finished product, distribution, and accounts payable.

2. Does this project extend back into the supplier's operation, and/or is the raw material pile included? Theoretically, the size of the raw material pile is a reflection of how reliable the vendor is. If you want to shrink the pile, you must improve the vendor. (Simply forcing material out of your pile and back into the vendor's pile doesn't really improve the overall environment; the cost of the supplier's increased internal inventory will inevitably be reflected in costs to you.)

3. Similarly, is the final product distribution system within the scope, and/or is customer service improvement an objective? Delivery and warehousing probably reflect reliability of the production operation. If you wish to speed or shrink the distribution system, you probably will have to improve the plant internals. Similarly, if you improve the plant responsiveness, you would expect to see distribution shrink.

4. Does this project include support functions? For example, is there a staff-level scheduling and/or an inventory control group? If you are going to work on improving the plant internals, one of the things you will want to do is to move control/responsibility *closer* to the floor operation. Self-scheduling systems and automatic inventory controls will be part of the new system. That will prove impossible to implement unless the scheduling function is known to be *inside* the boundaries from the start. Equally valid inclusion questions involve the maintenance organization, the QC lab, and the IS function.

5. Are all products included, or is this project limited to specific products? Generally speaking, it is difficult to operate part-time in a Time mode and part-time in a BAU mode. Therefore, if an area or piece of equipment is going to operate *at all* in a Time mode, all products that move through that point must be handled in a Time mode.

6. Are all parts of the physical process included? Limitations/exclusions could be either vertical or horizontal. As we move through the process, we might include some areas and exclude others. Or, within an area, some process units might be in and others out. This question tends to get answered in tandem with the product limitation question, and the answer is strongly influenced by the fact that anything that is going to operate at all in the Time mode probably has to operate exclusively in a Time mode.

Developing a Rollout Plan

Probably, the defined scope of a Time project implementation will be less than the full business, complete supply chain scope. Some portions of the product line will be excluded, portions of the supply chain will be out of bounds, some segments of the manufacturing process may not be included, and support organizations may or may not be included. In multiple plant situations, Time implementation will certainly start within one core plant. An up-front plan to extend Time backward and forward through the supply chain, through the product line, and through the full scope of the manufacturing operation is important. The plan may include an intent to extend Time to vendors and or to customers. That plan will influence makeup of the Core Team itself.

The general consideration is to take advantage of the initial project to develop leadership for following projects. As noted earlier, although these concepts can seem to be straightforward, it is difficult to appreciate or internalize the Time thought process, until you have experienced it as a member of a functioning team. That is the reason that the initial team needs an outside consultant: to ask the dumb questions that need to be asked, to challenge conventional thinking, to ask why questions, so that and until the minds of the team members open up to Time principles.

If you can salt your initial Core Team with people who will be leaders of following projects, you will have anticipated and resolved the question of who will facilitate that mind-opening process for the following teams. And you will have precluded the need for an outside consultant.

But a word of caution. In Du Pont, our problem was how to extend Time through approximately 150 locations quickly. Our initial thinking was that we would create clusters of plants, we would facilitate the initial plant, that we would salt that team with potential leaders from the other plants in the cluster, and that those people would return to their plants as leaders for their teams. The problem, however, was that it was difficult for people who had grown up in a specific product culture to be change agents for that culture. It worked much better when we created geographic clusters and sent, for example, a paint person who had experienced Time to then be a change agent in a fibers plant.

So plan your rollout so that you can use people who have gained experience in the initial project to be leaders or change agents in following projects, and be sure that those change agents can be effective in the project that they are expected to lead.

The Core Team Facilities

Part of the organizational Core Team considerations is providing the physical facilities they'll need. The ideal is as follows:

- A meeting room big enough for the team and for holding review meetings with area people, the Steering Team, and/or with the extended Core Team. That suggests potential to seat approximately 20 people. (It is difficult or impractical to hold those review meetings elsewhere because the meeting room walls will literally be papered with information that is needed in the review meetings.)
- Adjacent office space for members. Only the Core Team Leader office needs to be private.
- Availability of a part-time secretary for reports, graphics, and so on.
- Computer equipment for reporting, graphics, and for simulation modeling if that is to be part of the effort.
- Wall surface in the meeting room adequate for posting all maps and all opportunities. (Maps can grow to brown paper 3 feet wide by 10 to 20 feet long, and several hundred opportunities may be listed on flip chart paper.)

The Consultant

Do you need a consultant to pursue a Time activity? The answer is "That depends," and it depends on the following:

- The consultant *is* an expert on the Time thought process.
- The consultant's role is *not* to do the work.
- The consultant's role *is* to:
Transfer the technology to you.
Enforce the discipline of the process.
Ask the dumb questions that you won't ask.

The usual problem that people have in applying Time is a rush to judgment; they have spent 30 years getting to where they are, and suddenly they are impatient with taking a few months to carefully plan where they want to be and how to get there. The first day of the effort, when they see the first opportunity, they want to rush off and implement. (And there is absolutely no assurance that the *first* opportunity is also the best opportunity!) Or when the team has been together for a month and is partway into the mapping activity, management wants to know how much they've saved. Or, even worse, some new hot button appears and they want to reassign the team to the new fad.

So the first question concerning whether you do or do not need a consultant is a matter of whether you understand this thought process and have the discipline to enforce it. The consultant's role is to explain the thought process, in digestible bite sizes, and then to enforce the discipline of that process.

There is a typical shortcoming associated with the use of consultants. If the consultant serves to execute and implement a program or project that clients do not have resources to do themselves, then ownership of that activity resides with the consultant and leaves with the consultant. That is particularly true of a "thought-ware" activity like Time. Therefore, it is critical to the long-term ability of the Time activity to "stick," to become permanent, that the actual work be done by the people who are going to be living with and operating by the result. The resolution of the problem of finding resources to staff a Time team is *not* to do it by hiring consultants! The consultant only provides the *process* for doing the work and enforces the discipline of doing the work as it is laid out.

Discipline is not a trivial consideration. It is very difficult to understand a Time project until you have lived through and experienced it once. The process seems obvious and simple. There is a strong tendency to go too fast, to be too superficial, and to not ask the probing questions that are necessary. That is the prime role of the consultant: to hold back the process, to make the team ask the important questions, and to be sure that the critical answers have been reached.

The questioning nature that the consultant can bring to the process is a second important consideration. Team members are biased by their own experiences. They are so used to seeing things as they have always seen them that they are not able to challenge the current state. They will not see waste activities as waste, and they will not see alternative ways of doing things. The consultant, however, is not bound by his/her experience and is free to ask "Why do you do that?" Moreover, the consultant will ask that question over and over—until you get angry, until you realize that you are angry because you don't have a good answer, until your mind opens up to the fact that there is an opportunity to improve that you have been blinded to by your experience or your paradigms.

Until you have been through a Time experience, your mind is not open to recognizing opportunity, and that is a *major* reason for the consultant: to sense the opportunity and to guide you through the questioning process and open your mind to the future. In an ideal state, you would like the Core Team Leader to be the enforcer of discipline and the rigorous questioner. But, if he or she hasn't been through a Time experience, it is unlikely that the Leader will be able to do that.

So, in a perfect world, my answer to the question of whether you need an external consultant would depend on whether you had developed an internal ability to observe the discipline of this process and to ask the challenging (dumb) questions that need to be asked. If you haven't been through a Time experience yet, you probably don't have that ability. Don't let that deter you; at worst it just means your benefits will be smaller and/or will come more slowly. At best, I may be able to put you in touch with someone who has been through the experience and is willing to share.

The Implementation Team

A formal transition occurs from the planning phase conducted by the Core Team to the implementation phase. That transition is marked by formal presentation to the Steering Team of a Business Assessment and Improvement Plan. That plan includes what is to be changed, resources (people and money) required for the change, timing, and benefits (dollars and changes in the targeted metrics) expected. Although the Steering Team should be informed all along the way, this plan is the formal hand-off. The Steering Team advises, consents, and resources the next phase.

The basic Core Team will carry the project through the study phase—mapping, modeling, assessing opportunities, planning the general outline of how the operation is to be changed, and presenting the plan to the Steering Team for approval to move to implementation. Up to that point, it is at least possible (*decidedly* not desirable) that the team could be part-time.

At this point, the Core Team will be renamed, and perhaps substantially revised, into the Implementation Team. As you move into implementation, effort *must* be full-time. It just isn't possible to implement fast enough on a part-time basis; your environment will be changing or evolving faster than you can react to that change. Therefore, one way the team must change as you move to implementation is to ensure full-time participation.

The second possible change in the team is around ownership and acceptance. If you are to change the way the shop operates, it is imperative that you have ownership and acceptance of the change by the shop floor. The best (only?) way to get that is if the shop floor itself implements the change.

If the Core Team did not already have significant shop floor representation, it will have to be revised or expanded at this point. The exact nature of how you accomplish hourly participation in the new Implementation Team will depend on your own circumstances, but it is a primary issue and concern that must be carefully addressed by the Steering Team.

The tasks of the Implementation Team are:

1. Flesh out the details of all the changes. This could include considerations for such things as:
   - Pull Scheduling.
   - Group Technology.
   - The operator's part in continuous improvement (the ongoing management process that will be created for capture or identification of detractors by the shop floor people and for the root cause and pareto analysis work leading to correction/improvement; covered in detail in Section 5).
   - Rationalization of paperwork to avoid any duplication of effort introduced by Pull or continuous improvement.
   - Any changes in maintenance practices if that is needed to reduce Cycle Time.
   - Any operator involvement in SPC if process instability or quality is found to be critical.
   - Changes in QC lab procedures.
2. Complete the planning by surveying partners on the floor and being sure that floor ideas and concerns are blended into the final plan. Nothing contributes more to an operator's acceptance than seeing his or her ideas in the plan.
3. Educate the workforce in the theory of cycle time and in the specific changes planned. A one-hour to four-hour class session for every worker is usually necessary.
4. Dry run the changes on the floor before full conversion. Observe problems and make revisions as necessary.
5. Staff the transition. There is usually a single day identified as "Turn-On" day; it is a big-bang event that is carefully anticipated and marks the start-up of new systems and procedures. For a period (about 1–2 weeks?) the new systems need to be covered on a full-time basis by members of the Implementation Team. That coverage is to
   - Act as an observer and resource on the floor and help the people and the new systems over the initial rough spots.
   - Revise all documentation as necessary. The team should not

only be prepared to accept revisions, they should actively solicit revisions. (Inclusion of the shop floor builds ownership.)

First-Line Supervision

The initial diagram in this section depicting the entire Time organization shows the Implementation Team reporting jointly to the Core Team and to first-line supervision. That is to emphasize the absolute importance of gaining acceptance and active support of the first-line supervision.

Acceptance by the first line is often more difficult to achieve than is acceptance by the hourly roll. Because you will be implementing systems that empower the shop floor, no one is asked to change more than the traditional first-line supervisor. The BAU environment is one where the worker is told to "park your brains at the door ... the boss will tell you what to do." It is an environment where the supervisor can be an absolute authority. In contrast, a Time environment is very different and can be very threatening to that person. You'll need to work hard to gain this position's support, and if you don't have that support, first-line supervisors can be very damaging to your efforts.

Gaining first-line support begins long before implementation. First-line supervisors should be in on initial training and consulted often during the analysis and planning phases. As you are building maps and models, that work should be checked with the first line frequently. As you begin to assess opportunities and convert that long list into a focused plan, the first line should be involved. When you are preparing the Business Assessment for the Steering Team, a dry run should be done with the first line to get contributions and thereby support. Thus, by the time you get to implementation, the first line should already be well informed and involved.

As shown, the actual implementation should be jointly managed, by the team and by the first line. The team has all the technical detail; the first line has access to the real-world shop floor. This comanage-

> It is critical to get the Steering Team in place and functioning, before you initiate the Core Team work.

ment usually takes the form of one first-line person who is pulled out of his or her regular assignment and goes full-time with implementation for a period beginning after the Business Assessment is accepted by the Steering Team, extending through Turn-On (2–3 months), and ending after a period of run-in (about 1 month).

Summary: Organization and Metrics

What I've given you in this section is the Time process as applied to the classical full-blown organization. Almost every specific organization is different in some nuance dictated by a special case. But the basic structure is always there.

The biggest single failing that I have seen is not being rigorous enough about the Steering Team. Too often, this is viewed as a shop floor activity, and the thought and work begins there. As I've stressed, if you do that you may get wonderful plans, but if you have not altered the thinking and behavior of the business level, the unchanging behavior of management will cancel the changes you attempt on the floor.

The second failing is to attempt to implement with part-time people. This work constitutes major and basic culture change that is bigger and more fundamental than people realize until they find that they have been floundering for months, unable to get a firm enough fix on current state and on opportunities to be able to plan for a better future state.

> Part-time teams are possible, but they will cost you significantly in reduced benefits and extended implementation time.

How Will We Know When We're Done?

As with all sections, I close with a checklist of items to be completed before moving into the hard Core Team work covered in the remaining sections. You'll have more assurance of success if you are *ruthlessly rigorous* about completing this section before rushing into the next. When you can say yes to all of the items in this checklist, please proceed to Sections 3 and 4, which will be considered simultaneously.

Checklist: Am I Done?

- Steering Team is organized and meeting.
  - — All business functions represented
  - — Meetings on a regular distinct schedule
  - — Policy on attendance: in person vs. by phone/fax
- The organization of the full Time project is planned.
- General project scope or boundaries defined (the Core Team will have license to recommend scope modifications as they study the question).
- Core Team Leader and members identified.
- Decisions on full- or part-time made.
- A plan is in hand to free up team members for this assignment.
- A plan for expanding the team in the implementation phase has been made.
- A general strategy about expansion or extension of this effort to other areas or to other plants has been developed.
- Physical facilities planned and available.
- Strategic direction has been established in each segment of a balanced scorecard. Tactics in support of each strategy have been communicated to the management level and to the Core Team.

SECTION 3

Assessing and Planning

The definition of insanity is doing
the same things you've always done ...
and expecting different results.

—*Anonymous*

CHAPTER 9

Getting Started with the Core Team

The execution of Section 2 in this book should have provided the following: formulation of a Core Team including the designation of a Core Team Leader, provision for a meeting room and support services, definition of the scope and boundaries of this study, and, most important, a definition of the performance metrics that the team is to drive and to improve.

This section will now take you through a major portion of Time process: gaining an understanding of the operation, building a plan for change, and, most important, selling that plan to the Steering Team.

The topics we'll cover in Section 3, and the time it should take to execute the steps (assuming you have constructed a full-time team) are:

- Getting organized (1 – 2 weeks)
- Mapping/understanding the operation (4 – 6 weeks). This includes:
  The mapping operation itself
  Validating the map with the larger organization
  Identifying waste and nonessentials in the map
  Listing opportunities for improvement

- Simulation modeling. An optional task that you may choose to conduct concurrently with mapping and will require additional personnel if undertaken.
- Opportunity assessment. Selecting what to do (2 weeks)
- Developing and selling a business plan (2 weeks)
- Organizing for the Implementation Phase

Organizing

As you get started, the following are some initial activation considerations:

1. Clarify organizational issues. These might include things like:
   - Meeting times. If not a full-time team, you will want to publish a regular schedule so that priority is established and other pressures don't get in the way. (Remember, my *strong* recommendation is for full-time teams.)
   - Special roles for members within the team. These may be permanent roles for individuals or you may choose to rotate these assignments through the group. Special roles could include such things as:
     Scribe—the person who captures ideas as the meetings progress. "Capture" is usually either on flip chart paper or on whiteboards (boards that are capable of making 8½-by-11-inch copies)
     Secretary.
     Liaison to first line, liaison to hourly workers, liaison to other functioning teams. (If other teams are active, and if their efforts are liable to overlap your team's work in any way, it is important to maintain contact and to try for synergy of the two activities.)
     Opportunity Watchdog. As you are discussing *how* things are currently done, it is easy to miss passing comments that represent opportunities for improvement. These comments

may be in the form of actual improvement suggestions or they may just represent frustration about the problems with current practice. Either way, the comment reflects an opportunity and is important to capture. It is often very effective to have someone specifically assigned to listen for opportunities.

Social Director. If this team is going to *work* effectively together, it is a good idea that they *play* together as well.

2. Explain rules for conduct during the meetings. Our usual practice is to devote the first meeting to generating ground rules for the team. These are then posted and can be pointed out if someone violates. Typical rules include: be on time, no rank in the room, no idea is a bad idea, no question is a dumb question, loud isn't right, no personal attacks, volunteering is better than assigning, and so on.

Training

3. Begin initial training. Training might include:
   - Reading. Section 1 of this book would be a good training starting point. Also *required* reading is *The Goal*, by Eli Goldratt. You'll want to read and then discuss this landmark book. Other possible additions are *Synchronous Manufacturing* by Srikanth, *World Class Manufacturing* by Schonberger, and *America Can Compete* by Wantuck.
   - Metrics. The Core Team should discuss the metrics set for them by the Steering Team. The team should understand the how these metrics are measured and reported, and how the team may impact these metrics, as well as *why* they are strategic to the business. If the team does not feel charged up over the metrics, they will not make progress.
   - Process. All members will not be intimate with all parts of the manufacturing process. Overview process training at the start is important to get everyone on a somewhat equal basis.

- Other Teams. If there are other initiatives under way, one of the very early items is to sit down together and cross-train with the other teams and to look for ways that the two teams can ensure that they are supportive of and synergistic of each other.

With the initial training complete, the team moves immediately into the mapping process, which is the topic of the next chapter.

CHAPTER 10

Cycle Time Mapping

In this initial stage of a Time process, your team will build three types of maps: a Cycle Time map, an Operations map, and a Management Process map.

A Cycle Time Map

A Cycle Time map is the most straightforward and the easiest of the three maps to create. It is, as the name implies, a map of where Cycle Time resides in your process.

Remember the Cycle Time formula: $Ct = $ Inventory $/$ Demand. And remember that Cycle Time can be considered for the entire supply chain, from receipt of order to receipt of payment for the delivered product, or it can be considered for any component of that supply chain—a plant, an area within a plant, or a process unit within the area.

Remember also that I cannot enhance my Cycle Time by shoving material downstream to the next station. My Cycle Time is defined by all inventory between me and the downstream station; material inven-

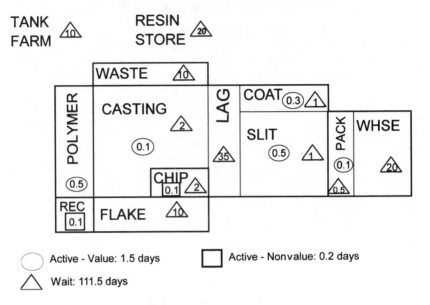

Figure 10.1 A Film Plant Cycle Time Map

tory counts against my responsibility until the downstream station actively pulls it in to work on it. So the complete map that you do should include distribution systems downstream of the plant with recognition that material in the distribution system may be there because of inadequacies within the plant.

So Cycle Time is essentially inventory levels expressed in terms of days of supply. And, a Cycle Time map is nothing more than a map of your process with inventory located on that map and expressed in terms of days supply. (See Figure 10.1.)

When you construct the map, you'll want to make some distinctions between types of inventory: active inventory being worked on versus inventory waiting, first-quality inventory versus restricted or off-

---

Box 10.1 An Inventory Proverb

- All inventory is there for a reason.
- To remove the inventory, you must remove the problem.

Box 10.2   An Inventory Corollary

■ If you remove the *reason* for inventory ...
■ The inventory will *vaporize!*

---

quality inventory, safety stock versus normal working inventory, inventory waiting for quality release, seasonal inventory, and so on.

A fundamental concerning Cycle Time and inventory is that all inventory is there for a reason. It is there because of some problem you have not recognized or are unable to fix, because of some policy you have set, because your systems are sloppy, and so on. You may not understand what that reason is, but the presence of inventory signifies that some problem, practice, or inefficiency exists.

You cannot effectively remove inventory without removing the problem (see Boxes 10.1 and 10.2). If you attempt to do so, one of two things will happen: either the inventory will return or you'll get killed by the problem you have exposed yourself to by removing the protecting inventory.

As you do this map, be sure that you are discussing and identifying the *reason* for the inventory. That may mean that you will have to segment a large single pile into several components in order to be specific about reasons. As you discuss reasons, that will naturally lead to discussions about opportunities to remove that inventory. Be sure to capture those opportunities. (Don't act on them yet, just capture them. See the discussion in Chapter 12 concerning opportunity management.)

Essentially coincident with building a Cycle Time map, your team will also develop an Operations map.

An Operations Map

This might alternatively be called a material flow map. What is entailed is identifying all action taken on material as it moves through the plant and all related activities that may influence how/when material does flow.

Mapping the operation is very much like progressive flybys: The initial view is from high up, and succeeding views are progressively lower and lower. The general ground rules on mapping are:

- The first view is from 40,000 feet; only six major blocks of the process can be seen.
- Each succeeding lower flyby provides a doubling of the process points that can be seen. One way this doubling of information might proceed is presented in Box 10.3.

In the mapping activity, consideration needs to be given to the following:

- **Documentation.** Each flyby needs to be captured so that it can be reviewed and upgraded by the larger organization and so that it can be preserved. Choices for documentation include drawing on brown butcher paper taped across the wall, drawing on overhead transparency paper (that can easily be displayed or projected later), drawing on whiteboards that allow you to print out copies, and/or PC software mapping programs.
- **Symbology.** The team needs to agree on a standard symbol set to use for the diagrams (see Figure 10.2 for an example). Any set will

---

Box 10.3   The Progressive Flybys of Time

First Pass—Six major buildings only
Second Pass—Major operational areas
Third Pass—Major process units (machines, vessels, etc.)
Fourth Pass—Inventory piles
Fifth Pass—Recycle/waste streams and machines
Sixth Pass—Inspection/testing practices
Seventh Pass—Informational practices (orders, scheduling, raw procurement, distribution methods)

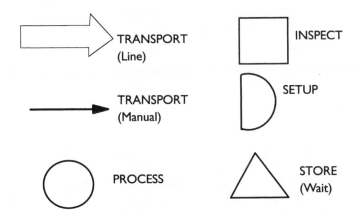

Figure 10.2   Standard Mapping Symbols

work, but the symbols used must distinguish value-add activities from waste activities.

One of the prime reasons for symbology is to make waste or nonvalue stand out. Of the symbols in Figure 10.2, only one *could* be value-add, the circle symbolizing an operation. Note: This does not *have to be* value-add. The operation could, for example, be a recovery or rework operation. In that case, it would not meet the test of value-add. But with these symbols you at least have a visual first-cut view of value in the operation versus waste trapped in the operation.

- **Identifying waste.** Beyond the symbols, as you make each flyby, identify each step clearly in terms of value-add or waste. Remember, *waste* is defined as anything the customer would not gladly pay for. On that basis, only physically changing the product in a way the customer values would qualify as value-add. Candidates for waste include counting, shuffling, sorting, reworking, transporting, testing, holding, and so on. There are two waste items on the list in Box 10.4 that people often question—testing and transportation. See Section 1 for a discussion. You may do the identification by color code, by stick-on labels, and so on. Whatever the choice, waste steps should be immediately obvious when looking at the map.

Box 10.4   Waste? Waste!

Holding   Testing
Counting   Sorting
Rework   Transporting
Transitioning

- **Identifying essential versus nonessential.** In addition to identifying waste, two subcategory distinctions are important to understand.

  Nonvalue and nonessential. What you want to find is nonvalue activities that are nonessential. When you find that, *you don't do that anymore!* Why would you ever find this combination? A common way involves testing where material is never rejected: "Dr. Jones asked for this data when we started, and no one has ever said to stop getting it."

  A real example of this is a plant that I audited which produced fiber-glass reinforced panels, the material you see used in patio roofs, for example. The process was a batch polymer operation that fed a continuous casting line. At the end of the line the continuous strip was chopped into discrete panels and packaged for shipment. At the end of that line was a person who did destructive testing on samples taken from the finished panels. I asked him what the failure rate was. His answer was "None. When it gets to the end of the line it always has good strength. The only cause for rejection is visual defects and I don't do that." When I asked why they tested when they never rejected, they looked at me like *I* was the stupid one!

  More likely, you will find the following.

  Nonvalue that is currently essential. Testing where reliability is poor is a good example. Most transportation is essential, given your current physical or geographic layout. Each nonvalue/essential step is an *opportunity!* If you can convert essential into nonessential (it may take time and effort to do that), you can then eliminate that step and simplify/speed the operation.

- **Identifying the bottleneck.** Eli Goldratt, in his book *The Goal*, has powerfully made the case for bottleneck identification and bottleneck management as being *the* critical manufacturing management paradigm. "Bottleneck" may refer to the single process step that is most fully loaded (operating at the highest percentage of capacity), or it may be a supporting function (the QC lab, for example) that blocks movement of material on the floor by slow or ineffective support service. Given that every process must have a definitive bottleneck, it follows that the most focused way to improve the operation of the whole is to focus on improvement of the bottleneck. (Goldratt argues that improvement anywhere *other* than at the bottleneck will not provide *any* overall improvement.)

  A special word about your bottleneck: If capacity utilization (actual output compared with maximum practical capability) is very high, you will have a special opportunity. We will discuss this in much greater detail in Section 4, but inventory that is required grows geometrically as capacity utilization grows, and workstations that are above 90% utilization tend to become unstable or unable to absorb surprises (see Box 10.5).

  Once one understands the bottleneck, it follows that your plan will include anything you need to do to protect and to optimize that bottleneck. That says a lot about where you position inventory, how you release orders into the system, how you control vendor actions, and so on. More will be said about this subject in Section 4. For now, be sure to have clarity about the bottleneck, identify things that act to detract from bottleneck performance (setup, downtime, yield losses), and be sure each detractor is balanced by an entry on your opportunities list.

Box 10.5   A Bottleneck Warning

- Inventory grows with increased utilization.
- Operation above 90% utilization creates instability or poor responsiveness to surprise.

- **Validation.** After each flyby, validation by others is important. *Validation* simply means bringing key people into the work room, walking them through the map, and capturing their comments and upgrades into the map. Key people include first-line supervision, other associated improvement teams, technical/engineering/ research people, and a good sampling of shop floor people. *It is very important that the validation process result in material changes to the map!* People will only be accepting of this process if they see their handprints on it. Fight off pride of authorship, and be very alert for opportunities to make additions/corrections to the map as you validate.

The end result of mapping will be a detailed map of material flow through the process, showing all setup, testing, transportation, inventory, and operational steps. All steps are identified as value-add or waste, and as essential or nonessential.

The last mapping variation is the Management Process map.

A Management Process Map

The Operations map (just finished) describes material movement through the operation. Sometimes the bottleneck to materials movement can be a management policy or practice, and that can be difficult to represent in an Operations map.

If you feel that your management practices are in any way suspect, you'll want to map those practices. The technique for doing that is sometimes called a "triple-diagonal" map;[21] I think the term Management Process map is more descriptive.

The map details three levels of management: the planning process, the execution of that plan, and the control of the deviations that occur (see Figure 10.3).

The key to this map is the control level. The detail of a control block shows the connection between the planning and the execution processes (see Figure 10.4).

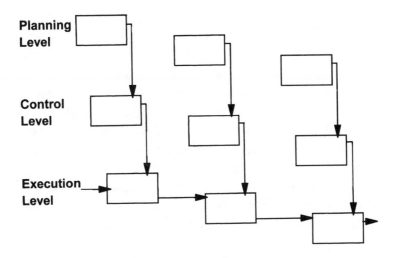

Figure 10.3 A Management Process Map

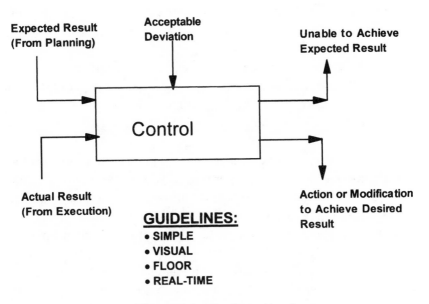

Figure 10.4 The Control Level

As you consider how to provide the control function for your operation, I'd like to suggest some guidelines: simple, visual, shop floor, common sense, operator owned, real time. (These are the same guidelines I would propose for almost all shop-floor activities.)

A good example of a control mechanism that meets our guidelines could be a Pull System. A planning process (perhaps MRP) is used to design the Pull System and its limits, and then the Pull System itself reacts to variations and warns us when there is danger of not achieving needed or expected results. See Section 4 for details on Pull.

In both the Operations map and the Management Process map, as we add each bit of detail, we are asking some key questions: "Why do we do it that way?" "Why don't we ...?" "Wouldn't it be great if we could ...?"

Those types of comments lead directly into identifying opportunities.

Opportunity Identification

Opportunity identification happens coincident with mapping. The ground rules are very much like any brainstorming activity:

- Assign a person charged with listening for opportunities as you map. Rotate this assignment every few hours. This person listens for opportunity comments. Opportunity comments take the form of "Why?" ... "Why not?" ... "Why can't we?" ... "Wouldn't it be nice if we could?" and so on.
- At every opportunity comment, the assigned person suspends the map work to capture the opportunity. Capture means nothing more than recording the item on flip chart paper that is posted on the walls around the work room.
- No attempt is made to qualify the opportunity. No estimate of benefit is made (yet).
- If the opportunity is a "wish," no final judgment is made about the feasibility of the opportunity. If you don't know how to accomplish the idea, it is still an opportunity and should be captured.

- No attempt is made (yet) to implement opportunities. *This is difficult!* It is easy to get excited and want to charge out and get results. But one of our prime principles is to *focus*, and you don't know what are the best ideas until you know that you have all the ideas.

I will qualify this last point somewhat. Some of my associates like to talk about "low hanging fruit." That describes something that is so juicy and so easy that you would just go ahead and pluck it. There may be some of that, and if there is you shouldn't turn away from the chance to make a strong impression early. Just make sure that you don't get sidetracked and that the assessment process doesn't get held up. "Low hanging fruit" takes no team distraction to eat!

It is typical that teams record several hundred opportunities during the mapping operation. In my experience, compiling 300 to 400 opportunities (big, small, practical or impractical) is normal. The record is 1,100! An allied activity that can aid understanding and add to the opportunity list is simulation modeling, the topic of the next chapter.

CHAPTER 11

Simulation Modeling

As with everything else in the area of computer technology, amazing advances have occurred in simulation software. Ten years ago, mainframe computers were required for any type of detailed process simulation. Five years ago, simulation was possible on a desktop PC via software packages costing $20,000. Today, simulation can be done on your laptop, and reasonable software packages are under $1,500. Moreover, advanced programming skills are no longer necessary.

A number of simulation packages are available. The one I use and recommend is Extend,™ offered by a company called Imagine That (San Jose, California). Extend™ is essentially a large library of icons that can be strung together to represent a work process, a paperwork process, a logic operation, or even an evolutionary process (fire generation, pollution spread, disease epidemics, etc.). Each icon, when double-clicked, has a dialog box that allows the modeler to specify the details of the icon's operation. Simulations can be either discrete event or continuous, data can be plotted, simulations can be animated, and submodels can be condensed into hierarchical single blocks within larger models. (A reactor with complex scheduling and quality rules can require hundreds of icon blocks to model, but then can be collapsed into a single block in a larger model.)

Extend™ has its limits. Storage/speed limitations will mean that you may not be able to include all the complexity of your full operation. Product or process complexity may have to be limited. But, although you may have to simplify somewhat, you can usually approximate real life closely enough to learn what one needs to learn.

As an example of capability, I recently worked with a company whose model involved 30 final products processed in a widely varying sequence through four distinct process steps. About 8 MB of RAM were required and a simulation run representing one year of operation took one hour on a 90 megahertz machine.

There are at least four good reasons to consider modeling:

1. Modeling forces you to understand your current operation.
2. A model allows you to play "what if" concerning the future without committing your actual operation.
3. A model is a useful tool for training.
4. A model is useful in justifying or selling change.

Modeling the Current State

The first modeling activity is to build a model of the way things are today. What *always* results is that the model you build runs *better* than real life—better yields, lower inventory, better service, higher capacity, and so on. That is not because the model is wrong, it is because you don't understand your current state. What is really happening out on the shop floor is not what appears in your operating manuals. To make the model look like the real world, it is necessary to go out, root around, talk to people, and find out what is *really* going on. As you find

---

The effort to make the model reflect the real world will force you to understand the real world ... and will generate ideas on how to improve that real world.

out how reality is different from theory, you will ask a lot of "Why do we do that?" questions, and that will generate many additional opportunities for improvement.

Playing "What If" about the Future State

Once you have a model that reflects the current state, you can drop changes into that model and look at what the future would be like with that change in place. Often, the impact of a discrete change somewhere within the system on the output or performance of the entire system is not obvious. Impact of capacity gains on customer service levels, for example, is not always direct cause/effect (if you are improving a nonbottleneck step, for example). In this way, you can use the model to qualify the impact of some of your opportunities that you have generated.

Justifying Change

With models built that show both current state and the proposed future state, justifying and selling that future state is much easier. The model will give you data tables and graphs to illustrate the benefit and may be visual enough to show the benefit dramatically. (Things like inventory piling up behind a bottleneck, orders queuing up, or idle workers can show up very dramatically in a model.)

Training

A working model can be very helpful in orienting new people, from first-line supervisors through business team members.

Examples: Good and Bad

A "Good" Example

One of the best examples I can give involved one of our major national companies, at one of their resin manufacturing sites. The process (see Figure 11.1) involved reactors that produced the basic polymeric material, followed by extruders that added the "wiffle dust" that gave final properties to the product. There were a handful of basic polymers and hundreds of final SKUs—a typical diverging process operation.

Because there were severe constraints on inventories, the Finishing operation generally ran on the basis of whatever base materials were available to finish and "pushed" that material into the finished product distribution system in the certain knowledge that "they'll sell it sooner or later." The result was low plant work-in-process (WIP) inventory, *huge* finished product inventory, and poor customer service.

Conventional cycle time analysis made the situation obvious. Cycle Time through distribution was more than 80 days and Value Time in the operation was only a few hours, resulting in an MCE of

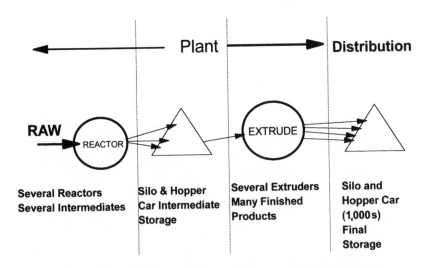

Figure 11.1 An Example Resin Process

less than 1.0. Further, when we began to look at the design for a Pull System (product wheels timed to match capacity to sales and the resultant defined inventory structure; see Section 4 for details on these techniques), it was obvious that the system had much more inventory than necessary. Most of that inventory (and Cycle Time) resided in the distribution system, but the *cause* of that inventory was lack of confidence in the plant's ability to deliver. What we had was a classic self-fulfilling prophecy, and/or a condition that was determined by policy instead of latent capability. The policy had squeezed down on in-plant inventory, ensuring that the plant would not be able to produce specific finished products as necessary. As the plant demonstrated that inability, scheduling/distribution people gained value for just-in-case finished inventory.

Our recommendation was to remove the constraints on internal inventory, operate to ensure that all variations of intermediate would be available to Finishing as needed, allowing Finishing to run to direct order. Our projection was that this would save several million dollars in overall inventory, lower cost, and provide better customer service.

However, to implement the change required first building intermediate inventory before finished inventory could be collapsed, and that meant a large (several million dollars) up-front investment on the promise that later savings (estimated at $10M) would result.

The resolution was to model the operation with new scheduling rules and demonstrate on a PC that the concept would work, *before* we made the commitment on the floor.

A Second Example

A small catalytic resin manufacturer used a process diagrammed in Figure 11.2. The company produced approximately 30 product variations. The base product looped several times through Steps A and B and then passed through Steps C and D to final sales. Some variants went through Step A multiple times before proceeding, some variants bypassed Step B, some products started at Step C, and so on. But the basic problems were twofold:

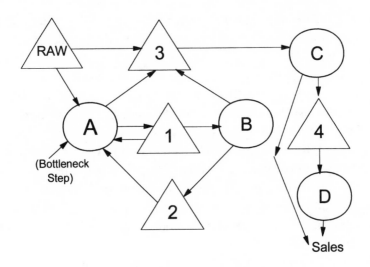

Figure 11.2 A Catalyst Process

1. Order receipt was extremely "lumpy." They received only 20 "events" per year, completely random in terms of product type, size, and urgency.
2. The first step was the effective bottleneck.

This type of process often exhibits the same type of problems as the classic bank teller queuing problem. Customers arrive randomly and queue up at a fixed capacity service point. The problem is to determine how many tellers are needed at various times of day in order to avoid building a line that angers customers and causes them to "flinch" (to leave).

In this case, given that huge orders arrived randomly and infrequently at a station at or near its maximum capacity, the bank teller problem was grown to nightmare proportions. The company wanted to submit a capacity expansion project (providing a second first-step unit) to their parent company but had difficulty demonstrating to the parent why a unit operating at less than 85% of nameplate annual capacity was insufficient.

A model was able to demonstrate the instability and inflexibility of the current facilities and showed the potential for increasing effective capacity while cutting interim inventories and improving service. The industry is service-critical, providing the probability of gaining overall share as well.

A "BAD" EXAMPLE

I recently worked with a small manufacturer of molded elastomer parts. Their basic process was as shown in Figure 11.3. An extrusion step converts raw materials into blanks, a wide variety (thousands of variations) of rough-formed O-rings in many thicknesses, diameters, and so on that are stored in a large bank. Cycle Time through that bank is about 30 days. Based on customer order, blanks are pulled from storage and put into heated molds (12 to 48 pieces in each mold) for final cure. Cycle Time in Cure is several hours. Parts exiting the mold have mold marks and flashing at seams that need to be removed in the next Buff operation. From there, 5% of parts are rejected and the rest go to Finishing for final inspection; yield loss there is approximately 50%. Cycle Time in Buff and in Finishing is approximately three days in each step.

Given the 50+% yield loss, the effective Cycle Time through this operation was approximately 90 days and, given a Value Time (Vt) of

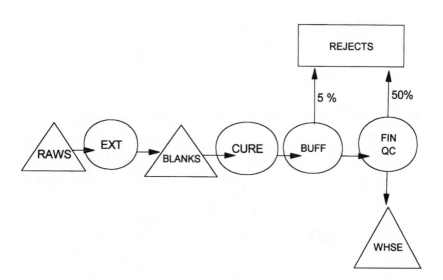

Figure 11.3 An Elastomer Parts Process

about a half-day, its MCE was about 0.5%. Management was very concerned and decided to model the operation to clarify what needed to be done to improve.

Figure 11.4 is the company's model of the Buff portion of its operation. This simple model includes a Resource block that acts as a holding tank, a Gate that opens when activated, and a Logic block that receives information about the amount held in the Resource block and makes a yes/no decision. The modeler has set this section so that the Resource block *must* hold three days of inventory.

When I asked about why the model was done this way, the answer was, "That's just the way it is." Obviously, no learning is taking place here, and no change is going to result. There are two factors at work:

1. There are *manufacturing* processes and *business/management* processes; you need to be clear on which one needs to be modeled. In this case, the problem is not the manufacturing process; it is the management/scheduling process.
2. In model building, you need to go deep enough into the detail to be sure you understand the why. In this case, all that has been done is to create a self-fulfilling prophecy—there will be three days of cycle time because "that's just the way it is."

This plant did get some value from the model effort because it illustrated the number of internal reorders generated by poor yields. To deal with Cycle Time concerns, the company realized that it needed to

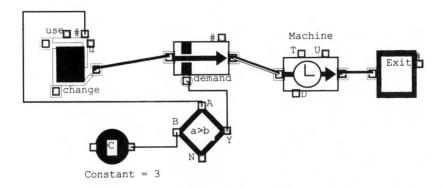

Figure 11.4 The Buff Model

address the way it managed the Buff and Finishing steps and shifted to doing a Management Process map (Chapter 10).

Making the Modeling Decision

Modeling is not for everyone, and it is a significant additional effort. The critical questions are:

- How well do we understand our operation? This is related to how predictably and stably the operation performs. The more unreliable and chaotic the operation is, the more there are likely to be aspects that are not well understood or that are different in actual practice from the documented practices.
- How likely are there to be multiple and conflicting solution paths to choose from? Will I have to make choices of action that are difficult to quantify?
- How tough is the selling job going to be? Will this be controversial? Will the commitment of resources (people or dollars) be painful?

If understanding is lacking, if the action decision is complex, and/ or if the solutions are costly or viewed to be risky, a model can be the critical component of the team's effort.

WHAT IS REQUIRED TO MODEL?

If you choose to model, the requirement is probably one additional person on the team. If your team already includes an information systems person, and if that person is not fully loaded, that might suffice. More likely, an additional person will be needed.

Qualifications for a modeler are more liberal than you might think. If you are using Extend™ or something similar, programming experience is not required. Models are not built by writing code, they are built by stringing blocks together into something in between a process diagram and a logic flow sheet. A logical, analytical mind and a bulldog work ethic are the main requirements. Because Extend™ is inexpensive, it is also quirky, and your modeler must be willing to suffer the frustrations of working through that. Formal training is not required, but classes (3–5 days) are available. Manuals for Extend™ are adequate, and a hot line is available.

If you were to work with P/TM in your project, we would provide all the modeling technical assistance that you will need. If you are going alone, you will suffer some modeling inefficiencies as you build your own capability, but that learning curve inefficiency is not a showstopper.

CHAPTER 12

Assessing
Opportunity

At this point, you have done the following and are about halfway through this segment of the process:

- Developed an understanding and appreciation for the performance metrics created by the Steering Team.
- Linked with other teams, with the first line, and with the shop floor.
- Identified where Cycle Time resides and why it is there.
- Mapped your process in considerable detail. The map includes identification of waste, and waste steps are categorized as essential or nonessential.
- Collected opportunities for improving the operation. If you've done this step right, you've papered the walls with opportunities. If opportunities don't number in the hundreds, you haven't done this carefully enough.
- *Perhaps* you have implemented some "low hanging fruit." You've done this only if it was easy and didn't interrupt the process.

The next step is to boil down the opportunity pool to the few focused options we will choose to actually pursue.

Box 12.1   The Seven Management Tools

■ Affinity Diagram
■ Relationship Diagram
■ Tree Diagram
■ Process Decision Program Chart
■ Arrow Diagram (The familiar PERT Chart)
■ Matrix Diagram
■ Matrix Data Analysis Grid

The Seven Management Tools

The tools for doing this are referred to as the Seven Management Tools (see Box 12.1).[22] These tools are to planning and managing as the Deming tools are to managing and improving quality. They are simple paper-and-pencil, commonsense tools for organizing and planning the improvement of the operation and the management process.

All of these tools might be put into use in the process of condensing a long opportunity list into a tight and comprehensive improvement plan. Here is one way that the process might go.

- *Matrix Diagram.* A Matrix Diagram (see Figure 12.1) is used to display lists of ideas to clarify relationships among them, or to segregate subsets of items. In our case, they are used to relate opportunities to performance metrics and objectives set by the Steering Team. Since our objective is to satisfy Steering Team (and business) objectives, it makes sense that we are only going to pursue opportunities that track against those objectives. This matrix provides a formal and visual way to make the first reduction.
- *Matrix Data Analysis Chart.* The general use for this chart is to map data or information into subsets or clusters (see Figure 12.2). In our case, it is used to further filter opportunities according to their practicality. Here we are mapping opportunities according to their

	OBJ 1	OBJ 2	OBJ 3	OBJ 4
OPP 1	●			
OPP 2			○	
OPP 3		●		
OPP 4				○
OPP 5			◉	

● Strong　◉ Moderate　○ Weak

Figure 12.1　A Matrix Diagram

impact and *feasibility:* how probable is success, and how big is the payoff. For those opportunities that tracked well against the performance metrics, a gross estimate of these two parameters are made, and the opportunity is then placed into the grid.

What we are looking for is obvious: high-impact ideas that carry a high probability of success. Without question, we will include those in

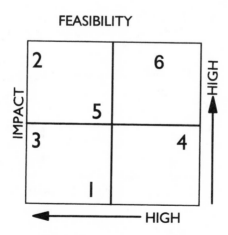

Figure 12.2　Matrix Data Analysis

our improvement plan. Low-impact ideas, feasible or not, will be dropped.

The intriguing grouping is high-impact ideas that are not currently practical (opportunity #6 in the grid, for example). The important point is how to move these items straight west; how to convert them from improbable to probable. The tool for that is a Tree Diagram.

- *Tree Diagram.* These diagrams are used to develop an action plan for accomplishing over time an objective that is not possible today (see Figure 12.3). The means for constructing this type of diagram is to start with an objective: *what* we want to accomplish. Then, ask two questions iteratively until an end point is reached. The questions are:

1. Can I accomplish this objective today? If not ...
2. What would we have to have in place to accomplish the objective? (Note that the answer may involve more than one requirement.)

The end point in this analysis is when you can say yes to the "Can I do this today?" question. In the example shown, the chart has branched into five requirements. If every one of those can be

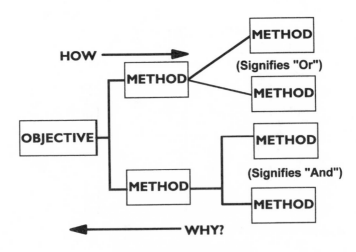

Figure 12.3 Tree Diagram

done today, the end of the analysis has been reached, and a plan for accomplishing the ultimate objective has been developed.

As one looks from left to right, the chart answers the question "How are we going to accomplish our objectives?" Each step to the right answers how the preceding step is to be reached. As one looks from right to left, the chart answers "Why are we going to do this?" Each step to the left is the goal or objective of the preceding step(s).

The result is a plan for shifting high-impact opportunities toward higher probability of success. With that, they can be included in the final improvement plan that your team develops and presents. All that is left in order to have a complete and actionable plan for this opportunity is to add accountability—specific responsible names and target dates—to each block on the chart.

The end result of the preceding is to focus on the specific opportunities you choose to pursue. The final steps are to develop an overall plan. For that, we'll use an Affinity Diagram.

- *Affinity Diagram.* These diagrams are used for grouping unorganized ideas into a structure of related concepts (see Figure 12.4). For our purpose, the Affinity process is to condense opportunities into a coordinated plan.

The process for constructing an Affinity Diagram is to pin up 3-by-5-inch cards or Post-its to record each surviving opportunity. Those are put up on the wall by the team in logical groupings. No arguments are tolerated; if people disagree on which grouping a

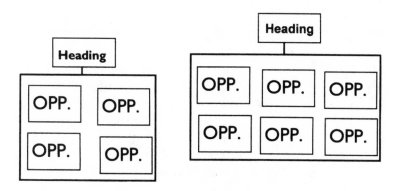

Figure 12.4 Affinity Diagram

specific idea belongs in, a copy is made and the idea is put in both groups. When all ideas have been posted, a header card containing the general idea of each group is created and posted.

If the process has condensed the ideas into a reasonable number of headers (approximately 10 major concepts, maybe as little as 5, and no more than 20), you are ready to move on to the next step. If not, the wall is cleared (keeping all the component cards of each group together), and the header cards are then posted in *their* logical groups, and new header cards are created for these groupings.

The grouping process may be done several times, if you have hundreds of ideas. You'll recognize when you have reached the optimum; too many cards and you can't see the logic, while too much grouping leaves you with an amorphous glob (see Figure 12.5).

When this process has reduced the opportunities into logical and manageable major groupings, you have gone a long way to create your final program: You now have major objectives, supported by all the detail tasks contained within those objectives. The remaining final task is to convert those stand-alone objectives into an integrated plan. The tool for that last step is the Relationship Diagram.

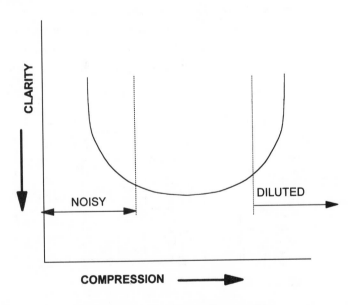

Figure 12.5 Condensing Opportunities

- *The Relationship Diagram.* This last tool is used to display complex interrelationships between ideas and to show cause-effect relationships. In our case, it is used to organize our major program objectives into a detailed plan (see Figure 12.6).

    The first step in creating this diagram is to post all the final header cards in a circle. Then, by drawing on the board or using connecting string, relationships are shown. Arrows are used to show cause-effect relationships, or which steps are dependent on others that must precede.

    When those relationships are shown, some few steps will have only arrows pointing *away*. These are key cause steps, and all else springs from them. Some (or one) will have only arrows pointing *toward* them. These are key effect steps and are the end result of all that come before.

    Experienced users will recognize that this stretched-out picture is very much like an arrow or PERT diagram. It shows a time-sequence of events and it is relatively easy to add specific date/time objectives to the diagram.

- *The Process Decision Program Chart.* As a last step, this chart (don't ask me why it has this pretentious name; I prefer to call it the Problem Planning Chart) is used to anticipate and plan for possible problems. It is visible contingency planning. (See Figure 12.7.)

    You'll want to build a chart for every major objective, and the method is simple. Starting with the objective, ask what problems might be encountered. For each problem, anticipate a fix. The fix

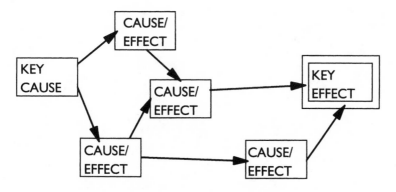

Figure 12.6 A Relationship Diagram

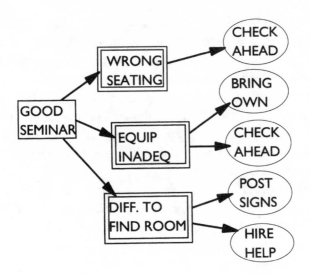

Figure 12.7 A Problem Planning Chart

itself might have potential problems, so the chart will require another level of fixes. Keep moving to the right until there are no unanticipated problems.

This step is *very* significant. You've taken a huge wish list of ideas and converted it into a hard-hitting and focused action plan. You've earned your pay for the year. Take a break!

CHAPTER 13

The Other Tools in the Toolbox

Up to now we've been working hard on an internal analysis of our operation and devising changes to improve and speed that operation. Now we want to consider what additional tools we want to include in our plan, to apply to our operation, in order to get more in initial up-front improvements and to strengthen the ongoing improvement process that we're going to put in place.

We'll divide this tool set and our discussion into two subsets:

- Standard world-class methodologies
- Special cycle time tools

In addition to defining these tools, or methods, a major purpose of this chapter is to show how a cycle time mentality *integrates* these tools and provides a logic for implementation.

Standard World-Class Tools

You know all of these, you love them, you can't live without them! You've certainly heard about some of them, and maybe all of them. You've probably tried to implement some, may have had good success with some, and I'm sure that a few of you have worked with every one of these.

The critical question is not what you've done, however, but what has translated to the bottom line. Many people answer that question: "Well, profits may look flat but things would have been much worse if we hadn't done this." Talk about "damning with faint praise."

But, first, what are we talking about? What do we include in this grouping? It is the standard list of acronyms: SMED, TPM, SPC/SQC, QFD, DOX, Six Sigma, TQM. (Make your own additions.)

SMED—SINGLE MINUTE EXCHANGE OF DIE

This is the technique of analyzing and improving the changeover or transition process. It generally consists of three phases.

1. Cataloging changeover steps. This is usually done by videotaping the operation, which can be hilarious as many minutes of tape go by with the machine down and no one in view while people hunt for tools, wait for lockouts, or simply wait for needed people to arrive.
2. Separating the total job into internal and external steps; *internal* steps are those jobs that must be done while off production, and *external* steps are those that can be done either before the machine is shut down or after starting back up. Even this simple step can save major portions of the unimproved changeover by avoiding doing unnecessary work while the unit is down.
3. Simplifying internal steps. Here, the value of understanding the principles of value versus nonvalue comes sharply into play. If a nut must be tightened on a bolt, only the last turn has value. If

something must be moved, all of that move is a target for simplification. Things like quick disconnect couplings, specialized tools that are color coded in the same color as their point of use, parts that will fit together only one way, detailed process settings, and so on are very effective in tightening up these steps.

TPM—Total Productive Maintenance

This is a combination of two preceding maintenance methods.

1. Preventive maintenance. The recognition that equipment had probable failure rates and the scheduling of overhaul or replacement before that failure occurs.
2. Predictive maintenance. Analytical techniques, such as vibration analysis and recovered lubrication oils testing (for metal content) to detect actual failure in the infant stages so that time between overhauls can be maximized without the risk of an actual failure.

The primary metric under TPM is Uptime and looks at two factors: Is the unit running? and Is it running at standard rate? The parameter is penalized for anything that detracts from maximum throughput over the performance period.

Although a Time approach abhors the inefficiency of mechanical failure, I think you can guess why we might be concerned about an Uptime metric. (Can you say "unnecessary production"?)

SQC—Statistical Quality Control

The precursor to SPC, this is product quality testing (preferably on-line, in-area, by operations ... but usually in the QC lab). Results are plotted on a chart with statistically developed upper and lower limits; results outside the limits signal that the process output has shifted in a statistically significant amount. Process adjustment rules are very specific and are only allowed when limits are exceeded, operator tweaking by individual whim is not allowed, and the amount of the specific adjustment is usually well defined by the SQC system. It is well documented that this rigorous and disciplined approach produces tighter quality control compared with control by individual operator skill or intuition.

SPC—STATISTICAL PROCESS CONTROL

As just mentioned, SPC is the evolution from SQC. The concept is that, instead of measuring the product output and then reacting by adjusting the process, the preferred approach is to understand the process and the linkages to quality well enough that it is possible to specify and lock in the critical process parameters with confidence that the resultant output quality is assured.

One major outgrowth of either SPC or SQC is the ability to separate out *special* from *common* causes (see Figure 13.1). Common causes are internal causes of variation, those variations that are an inherent part of the process, as it stands today. Special causes are external causes of variation that impact on the process to shift it to a new center point (although the example in Figure 13.1 shows a major shift, special cause changes in process aim could be subtle).

People either do not understand common/special causes, or they blatantly misinterpret one for the other. One of my favorite examples

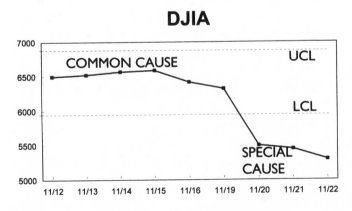

Figure 13.1 Understanding Cause

is the stock market. Only today, the Dow Jones average "plummeted" 42 points. The change is actually only about 0.5%, completely within the normal market noise, but the pundits will breathlessly tell you it was because of disappointing earnings from Company X.

The idea is that plotting your experience allows you to separate common from special causes. You then attack outside influences first and protect the operation from them. Only when you've isolated the process from outside disruptions can you go after improving the process itself. In my limited experience, eliminating external special causes is enough to put you where you need to be.

The obvious benefits of SPC versus SQC is that there is no hysteresis, that is, no time lag, in SPC; control is on-line and in real time. The not-so-obvious benefit is that SPC/SQC charting can be done by the floor and thereby involve them by giving them the tools to manage their own improvement. QFD and DOX can be looked at as subsets of the process of implementing SPC.

QFD—Quality Function Deployment

QFD represents the voice of the customer; it is the rigorous process of developing meaningful customer specs that both represent true customer need and that provide a durable competitive advantage.

The methods of QFD are far beyond the scope of this brief section, but the concepts and principles encompassed by QFD are vital to a Time approach. That criticality is best illustrated by the alternative.

Within Du Pont, we valued and viewed ourselves as an R&D company. What we did was invent the polymers, polyesters, explosives, films, fibers, petrochemicals, and so on and introduce them to the world. The quality approach was to invent, to design a manufacturing process, measure the output of that process, and use that quality distribution curve to set the quality limits. We then told the world "This is Nylon, these are the specs, take it ... you'll love it."

With that basis for setting specs, our response to improving output quality, to reducing the variation in output, was to tighten the specs. We worked at continually improving our customer specs. The obvious problem with that approach is that there is no connection with *true* customer need. Further, our actions *trained* the customer to extract anything/everything they could from us; we never realized any internal benefit from the gains that we made.

The better way is to start by defining true customer need in a partnership with the customer. (In complex situations, QFD is the means for doing that.) Then, with the customer understanding the shared benefit potentials, it is possible to freeze customer specs as the process is continually improved so that the improvement can be reflected in reduced cost and improved yield/productivity.

DOX—DESIGN OF EXPERIMENTS

DOX is the statistical process for linking process control parameters to product quality results; residual shrinkage in film is related to the amount of orientation (stretch) in the casting process, film temperatures in the casting oven, and time exposure to final oven heat-set temperatures. DOX is critical in moving from SQC to SPC as it allows confidence in resulting quality in response to rigorously setting process conditions.

SIX SIGMA

This is nothing more than SPC/SQC, under the discipline of a special metric, Process Capability Index (Cp). In its simpler form, Cp is defined as:

$$Cp = \text{Quality Spec Width/Process Variability}$$
$$\text{or}$$
$$= \text{(Upper Spec Limit} - \text{Lower Spec Limit)}/6\sigma$$

(6σ refers to the statistical range of quality variation and covers 99.7% of the product output.) See Figure 13.2.

Typically, as mentioned, our classical Du Pont approach was to set specs equal to our statistical measure of process output (Cp = 1). There

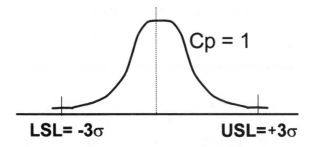

Figure 13.2 Capability Index

are two problems with that: There is no connection to true customer need, and waste is *guaranteed*.

All processes have long-term time variation; after you have carefully and statistically measured output, there will be drift over time. If specs have been set to observed limits, there is assurance that there *will* be yield loss. (In the case of normal statistical distribution the typical long-term drift is +/− 1.5σ, and the resultant yield loss will be about 7%. Sound familiar?)

The Six Sigma approach drives for a Capability Index of not 1, but 2. This is not achieved by forcing spec width *out*. It is achieved by setting specs (by QFD) to true need and then, in partnership with customers who understand the shared benefits, the specs are left stable while process variability is driven down within. See Figure 13.3.

This brings us to the most discussed and most misunderstood of the world-class tools: TQM.

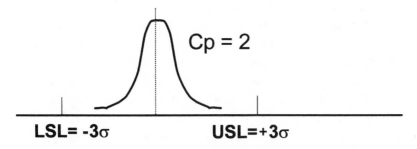

Figure 13.3 A Robust Process

TQM—TOTAL QUALITY MANAGEMENT

There are almost as many variations of TQM as there are claimed practitioners. And you'll have to allow me some personal bias and hyperbole in this discussion.

That said ... TQM is a concept or philosophy, not a technique. It is all the tools in the toolbox, without a vehicle for implementation. Or, worse, it is the idea that we are going to use/apply *all* the tools, all at the same time.

You've already read often in this book about my concern for focus; you can't fix everything at once, and you can't chase all fads simultaneously. You somehow have to choose what is critical to your situation ... at this time.

This brings us (at last) to the question of how a Time cycle time approach results in, or provides, the integration of these tools.

Integrating the Tools Via Cycle Time

In a nutshell, a Time approach is the implementation method that TQM lacks.

You have just mapped the operation and have identified waste. You have also done a Ct map and have identified the reasons or causes for the presence of nonvalue time. Being able to quantify time in the process, to segregate nonvalue time from the total, and to be specific about the cause of that time is a very powerful position, and it makes the necessary tool(s) obvious.

Remember that cycle time is simply inventory expressed as time. In Section 4 as we discuss building Pull Scheduling Systems, we will identify five major factors in the determination of required inventory structures. Those are transition times, machine downtime, throughput rate through the machine when it is up and running, yield losses, and sales

---

Box 13.1 Cycle Time vs. TQM

The guide for choosing and implementing TQM tools is the understanding of which will have the biggest impact on reducing Cycle Time.

---

demand for the output. By understanding your own necessary inventory structure and the determining factors of that structure, you should be able to identify the world-class tool (or the *few* tools) that will have the biggest impact on extracting time from your own specific operation.

Here is a real-life example of how the approach presented in Boxes 13.1 and 13.2 can bring order and focus. At a paper mill plant, management felt a strong need to both reduce inventory and to improve customer service. Details of their operation were:

- Production cycle: approximately 85 days to cycle through production of all product variations on the single paper casting machine.
- Customer order Lead Time: 4 to 6 weeks. The target was to reduce this to two weeks.
- On-Time delivery: 65%. Target performance = 95%.
- Machine downtime: 10% for all causes.
- Yield loss downstream of paper machine: 20%.

Obviously, reaching its service objectives while also reducing inventory involved the company's being able to move through its production cycle much more quickly. When we first entered this plant,

---

Box 13.2 A TQM Corollary

We will pursue *no* TQM tool that will not have an immediate and major impact on Cycle Time.

Moral

Cycle Time = Focus

---

management had three teams commissioned: Transitions, Maintenance, and Yield Loss, and each was working diligently (and independently). We asked each team to estimate their ability to improve their assigned parameter. Through methods that we will cover in Section 4, we were able to estimate the impact of each individually on the overall production cycle. Here is that impact:

- Maintenance: 6-day reduction in the production cycle
- Transitions: 7-day reduction
- Yield Improvement: 67 *days* reduction in the cycle

Question: What do you think the likelihood is that the transition team could encourage quicker start-ups and thereby add to yield loss? What is the possibility that keeping equipment running longer could result in yield degradation?

Answer: We quickly disbanded Transition and Maintenance teams and focused the entire organization on quality/yield opportunities.

Time Core Tools

In addition to the TQM tools that you will selectively choose to use, there are some core cycle time tools that also likely will be part of your plan. Those are:

- Visible Management
- Group Technology
- Pull Scheduling

Pull Scheduling is a core Time tool, and Section 4 is devoted solely to that subject. Section 4 should be completed in conjunction with this section but before you complete the Business Plan discussed in the last chapter of this section.

VISIBLE MANAGEMENT

Visible Management is discussed in much more detail in Section 5, which covers continuous improvement. Basically, the intent is to make the status of the operation clearly visible to anyone observing that operation.

Each area will have some type of display board, either manually or electronically kept up to date. That board will show:

- What are we trying to make? The metric here is *Takt Rate*. As mentioned earlier, *takt* is a German word that translates to "beat of the music." In manufacturing, it refers to the desired production rate in terms of units of production per unit of time: 10 T/day ... 10 hopper cars/month.
- What are we actually achieving against that objective?
- If we aren't getting what we want to, why not? What is the problem?
- Who owns that problem? Who do we look to to fix it?
- When will it be fixed?

These displays serve the two purposes in Box 13.3.

Box 13.3   Visible Management

- To ensure that problems are managed in real time, on the shop floor, by shop floor people.
- To capture the true problems and feed those into our continuous improvement mill.

The primary considerations in laying out your Visible Management system will be:

1. How often will I reset Takt Rate? The Takt Rate exiting the plant will be fairly stable, resetting somewhere between weekly and monthly. If you have an overall MRP system, the plant will tie into the regeneration of a Master Production Schedule and Takt Rate will be reset accordingly. The desire is to have this exit rate as stable is possible, given the market situation.
2. How often will I report production against that Takt Rate? If the reporting interval is too long, it will be difficult/impossible to clearly identify the detractors. If production against takt is, for example, reported only once per day, there will be many detractors and people's opinion/emotion will enter into what is posted as a reason. (Each line entry on the Takt Board should identify one main reason only.) If the interval is too short, you'll get too much static or noise in your information, and you'll create enemies on the floor as well. Reporting intervals usually are somewhere between hourly and twice per shift.
3. Is this going to be redundant with existing paperwork? Part of setting up this type of system is to do a review of existing records and to rationalize that. Just like your analysis of the production, you'll want to look at each piece of paper and challenge whether it adds value, how the information is used, if that information is redundant elsewhere, and so on. Acceptance of the Visible Management Takt Board will be in part proportional to whether it introduces extra work or whether it simplifies work.

The end result of this type of system (discounting the continuous improvement aspect covered in Section 5) is the ability to quickly take the pulse of the operation. Results and needs are instantly and visibly obvious to anyone who wants to know.

GROUP TECHNOLOGY

In discrete manufacturing, Group Technology refers to cell manufacturing. In that environment, the opposite of cell manufacturing is a farm layout—all the drill presses in one department, the milling machines in another, and so on. Group Technology is the rearrangement of that equipment to produce a finished part in each cell—carburetors here, fuel pumps there, and so on.

In a process plant, rearranging into work cells is not a consideration; equipment is massive and permanent. In this environment, Group Technology refers to understanding and minimizing the alternative number of *routes* through the plant.

If a plant has several areas, and each area has multiple (and essentially identical) production units, then the total number of routes through the plant is the multiple of the number of units in each area. For example, if a plastics resins plant has three monomer reactors, two polymerizers, and four finishing extruders (for the addition of additives), then there are 24 alternative routes through that operation (see Figure 13.4).

In a BAU plant, flexibility through that operation is often valued highly, and the ability to produce all products by all routes is maintained. The hidden trap is that, if you have 24 routes for a product, you are essentially making 24 different products (identical equipment isn't *really* identical, operators don't operate identically). See Figure 13.5.

With a Group Technology approach, the value shifts 180 degrees to valuing the minimization of the number of routes to essentially valuing *inflexibility*. The method is to pareto (see Chapter 20 for further discussion of pareto) the product line and to assign the high-volume

3 x 2 X 4 = 24 ALTERNATE ROUTES

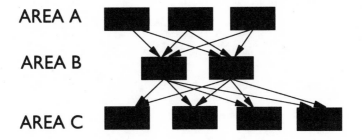

Figure 13.4   Group Technology

24 ROUTES MEANS...
24 PRODUCTS !

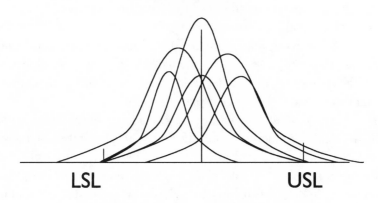

LSL   USL

Figure 13.5   The Flexibility Penalty

and/or competitively strategic products to single routes. The result is often that some routes will make only one product and/or one product will be made all the time through a particular route—no start/stop, no changeovers.

That is an *extremely* powerful position to be in. Now that you are making this product every day, there is no need for protective just-in-case inventory or for customer order Lead Time.

In practice, the result will be some routes that are like superhighways for critical products, and those will be highly tuned for that product. Other routes will be set up specifically for high flexibility to make all low-volume newstrategic products that remain.

CHAPTER 14

The Business Plan

At the start of this section, we promised a business plan that could be sold to the Steering Team. Based on the work you have now done, that is a piece of cake. Look at what you have:

- A detailed understanding of the process, including an Operations map with waste and nonessentials highlighted, and a Cycle Time map with reasons for time delay identified. These maps have been verified with hourly personnel, first-line supervision, and with other teams.
- A huge list of opportunities that has been pruned to the critical few that track most effectively against the performance metrics set by the Steering Team.
- A selection from the TQM toolbox of the tool(s) that can be most effective, most quickly, in your unique organization.
- A selection of the cycle time techniques needed in your operation.

All that is needed is to create the implementation plan and develop the expected benefits.

Benefits Estimates

I assume you have someone on the Core Team who understands the cost sheet, and therefore can estimate your plan's impact on it. But following are some general issues to consider.

CYCLE TIME OR INVENTORY REDUCTION

This divides into two components:

1. Onetime cash flow reduction. If you permanently reduce inventory, then you avoid (once) the cost of replacing that inventory. This will not show in a product manufacturing cost savings, but the actual out-of-pocket cost of providing inventory will show as a reduction in cash flow. This could be looked upon as cash available for capital projects.

2. Annual carrying-cost reduction. If you don't have inventory, then each year after that, you avoid the real cost of carrying that inventory. In the old BAU environment, this has usually been limited to the cost of money: If I invest $1.00 in inventory, then I don't have it to invest, and I lose the interest that I might have gotten. The BAU cost accountant usually values that at typical interest rates.

A more realistic accounting would include all the costs associated with inventory:

- "Interest rate" should be the hurdle rate at your company for approval of capital projects: 15%? 20%?
- Inventory requires space. What does space cost?
- What equipment is associated with handling/maintaining inventory?
- Do I handle inventory? What are the people costs?

- Do we experience inventory shrinkage? Does inventory get damaged? What is the shelf life? How about obsolescence? In total, what percentage of our inventory is lost each year?

Your estimate of your inventory carrying cost will depend on your type of manufacturing. If your inventory is stored in tanks, if you account for inventory by reading the level gauge, if there is no spoilage or obsolescence, if no labor will be saved by reducing inventory, then your carrying cost might be as little as 20% per year. On the other hand, if your inventory is 50-pound bags, if you handle it often and manually, if bags are broken, if product goes obsolete or has limited shelf life, then your annual cost of carrying that inventory might be as much as 40% per year.

CAPACITY OR MARKET SHARE

This can be the most attractive option you have. There are only two possibilities: either your capacity is sold out, or it isn't.

If you are sold out, then any increase in effective capacity translates immediately into incremental earnings. Incremental earnings means selling price less out-of-pocket costs for producing an incremental unit of production. In almost all cases, you already have the equipment, space, people, utility costs, and so on. All you need to spend for that additional product is the raw material costs. Further, if you think deeply about this option, increased capacity means increased share, which means reduced share for your competition, which cripples their ability to reinvest in their business, which means a continually strengthening competitive position for you.

The Most Significant Metric?

For the preceding reasons, some pundits maintain that you can stay competitive *only* by an annual increase in market share!

The only other option is that you are not sold out. Goldratt would say that you are limited by your *definition* of your market; his attitude is that all markets are unlimited (or limited only by your definition). If you accept that, then you have unused capacity due to something that limits your access to the market. And that can only be one of four things: price (which is the same as your cost), your product design or specifications, your quality conformance to those specifications, or your service to the customer. There *can't* be any other reason (except an incompetent sales force, which can be considered poor service), and all those reasons have a cause that resides within the plant (see Box 14.1).

So, sold out or not, your volume limitation—the denominator of the Ct formula—has a cause that is within the control of the plant. Whatever your case, an estimate of increased volume will provide significant financial rewards for your effort.

Box 14.1   A Market Limit Fable

I worked once with a plant that had *horrible* internal problems. They had no control of their process, no customer reliability, no concept (much less control) of their bottleneck, and their market share was low and decreasing.

One action was to formally identify the bottleneck. The plant had a formal ceremony and presented an eight ball to the manager of that operation. She worked and worked and eventually was able to call a meeting and transfer the eight ball to another portion of the plant.

Eventually, management got the plant in good control, got effective capacity up, and held a formal meeting where they presented the eight ball to the Sales Manager. What did the Sales Manager do? Turned around and presented it back to the plant in the form of better service needed to gain new business!

Yield Improvement

Certainly your opportunities have included some effort toward reduced rework or product loss. Be careful to not double-count these benefits. If you have taken credit for reduced inventory carrying cost, part of that may be reduced rework inventory because of improved yield. But improved raw material consumption is certainly fair game.

Employee Utilization

I am definitely *not* a fan of cutting people; they are your most valued resource. Some portion of your people are currently consumed in the waste activities of your operation. If your MCE (remember, MCE = Vt/Ct) is very low, your improvements will increase that, which means you are freeing up people. If those people are now available, what could they deliver in benefits from solving problems? Again, be careful not to double-count. If you have used a high percentage for annual inventory carrying cost, that improvement may have assumed reduction of people. You may want to reconsider and estimate the improvements that can be gained by having people free to tackle the tough problems.

Planning the Implementation Phase

Developing the business plan should take about three months. Following approval, you will move into the implementation phase, also requiring about three months. Implementation is the detail planning and get-ready step, and implementation ends with actual and major change in the way you do business on the floor.

In Section 2, the Steering Team was asked to anticipate implementation. They were left with two alternatives:

1. Carry on through implementation with the existing Core Team.
2. Expand to a broader Implementation Team that is more representative and/or includes more shop floor people.

In either case, you'll want to segment the Implementation Team and assign specific people to specific portions of the plan. Guidelines for implementation are:

- This period is to do the detail planning. Up to now you've developed concepts and general plans. Now the details of your Pull System, sizing of kanbans, laying out Visible Management Boards, doing detail Group Technology, and so on can be fleshed out.
- Plan to do basic cycle time education for everyone—at least a half-day on the general principles of why it is important. (You should be able to repeat the training you used to get your Core Team going.) You may want to educate on your specific plan also, but start with the basics.
- Don't surprise; allow plenty of time for covering the detail plan, individually or in small groups, with first line and with shop floor to get input.
- *Expect* to change the plan based on this input. In fact, be sure that you do. Ownership and acceptance will be much stronger if people can see their ideas used.
- Plan to lay out any shop floor plans and do dry runs well before you change for real. Take comments and blend them into the final plan.
- Plan for on-floor coverage on all shifts for the first week or two. *Expect* to adjust the plan.

Delivering the Plan

The format of the plan and its presentation is obvious. There are three sections:

1. Components of the plan. *What* do we propose to do?
2. Benefits of the plan. *Why* do we want to do this?
3. Implementation plan. *How* do we propose to do this? *Who* will do it? *When* will it be done? *What* will it cost?

For the actual presentation, have as much of the plan as possible presented by the people who will be using the result. This is not a top-down dictate of how things should be done; this is a plan by the shop floor for how they can work in a more effective, involved, empowered way. Ownership is built by their involvement in selling the plan.

The Road to a Business Plan

- An Operations map identifying waste and nonessentials
- A Cycle Time map locating time pools and their cause
- A listing of all opportunities for improvement
- A reduction of those opportunities to the critical few high-impact opportunities that track against the performance metrics set by the Steering Team
- A selection of the few TQM tools that track against your special needs
- A plan for use of Time tools including Pull, Group Technology, and Visible Management
- An estimate of benefits for the plan
- A detailed plan for implementing these opportunities, including steps to anticipate all possible negatives or objections
- And, finally, a successful presentation of the plan to the Steering Team

How Will We Know When We're Done?

This one is easy. You'll be done when you've sold your plan to the Steering Team. But the steps we've taken to make that sale are listed in the preceding box. This section's tasks are intended to be done in conjunction with those in Section 4, Pull Scheduling. When *both* have been completed (and not before), you are ready to set your process for ongoing continuous improvement via Section 5.

SECTION 4

Pull Scheduling

We will make no product before its time ...
and we'll make them come and get it!

—*Anonymous*

CHAPTER 15

The Pull Concept

One way to define Pull is to describe its alternative: Push Scheduling. Push is the traditional way a BAU organization does its scheduling. A sales forecast is developed, which is converted into production schedules for each area, and then each area runs as hard as it can against that schedule—"pushing" material downstream. Under Push, the definition of success is to have your downstream customer buried in product.

By now you should understand the fallacy in that method: Excess production equals waste activities and disconnection. Pull, however, intends to link stations together and to cause upstream to produce in response to downstream demand, to minimize time between the two, and to maximize connection.

The Origination of Pull

Pull was conceived by a Mr. Ohno of Toyota (you may have heard reference to the "Toyota Production System"). Have you heard people speak of an "Ah Ha" moment, the moment that a breakthrough idea registers? Mr. Ohno's moment came when viewing an American supermarket. Japan did not have supermarkets; it had mom-and-pop specialty stores on every corner. As Ohno was a scheduling/inventory/distribution person for Toyota, he was drawn to how supermarkets handle that problem. Read on . . .

Supermarkets manage by dividing up the shelf space by product—so much space for toothpaste, so much for carrots, so much for deter-

---

Box 15.1   The Corner Liquor Store

Until recently, I lived in center-city Wilmington, Delaware. Like most East Coast large cities, Wilmington is a mix of very nice restored areas and war zones. Sometimes the dividing line can be no more than a single street.

I won't tell you which I lived in, but I will tell you that at the border of my neighborhood there was a liquor store. To give you an idea of the quality of that store, if you wanted to buy a bottle of wine in that store, it was impossible to buy a bottle with a cork in it; only screw-cap wine was available. Further, if you bought a bottle, the assumption was that you were going to drink that bottle *right now,* maybe even before you left that store.

So the owner only sold chilled wine; he didn't offer an option. You chose your bottle from the shelves, he took that to his cooler and performed a switch for a cold one. And when he had extra time, he was not loading bottles into the cooler. That would be wasteful. He waited for me to make that purchase decision, made the switch, and then restocked his shelves each evening.

If the owner ever goes to that cooler to perform the switch and finds that he doesn't have a cold one ready, he adds a bottle to the cooler. Conversely, if he finds that he always has extra in the cooler, he takes one out.

He doesn't know it, but he is running that cooler on a very simple but very clever Pull System!

gent, and so on. And, when they have extra time, the warehouse people are not bringing in pallet loads of toilet paper and stacking them in the aisles; that would be wasteful. They wait for shelf space to empty, and that empty shelf space is *visible permission* to bring in more.

The classic supermarket example is the Frito-Lay delivery person. The market does not issue specific purchase orders but a blanket order to Frito-Lay. The store then allocates shelf space to Fritos®, based on demand and the attractiveness of the profit margin enjoyed. The driver then just shows up every day and refills the shelves. If demand goes up, the store just expands the shelf allocation and the delivery person reacts. Periodically, Frito-Lay sends an invoice. Given that simple powerful system, would you want to go back to forecasts and specific purchase orders?

Once you understand the concept of Pull, it's almost fun to look for everyday examples. Box 15.1 presents my favorite. Your assignment is to look around you and find your own Pull example.

Pull in Industry

The objective of Pull is to simplify the scheduling problem, to minimize time (inventory) in the operation, and to link stations closely together (to make cause/effect relationships visible). The classical Pull tool is *kanban*, typically a kanban square. In Japan, the term *kanban* has a dual meaning. Kanban refers both to inventory itself and to visible permission to produce. In this book, I'll keep it simple: When I mean "inventory" I'll say inventory and when I mean "permission to produce" I'll say kanban. (The Japanese root of *kanban* goes back to their word for "sign board.")

The kanban square is just that, a square painted on the floor or on the table between me (the producer) and you (the downstream user or next production station). The rules are simple: If there is space in the square, I have permission to produce; if there is not, there is some problem, and I must wait. Or, better yet, since there is some problem, I might as well go and see if I can help because I can't produce until space is cleared. (*Don't panic!* The purpose of Pull is *not* to shut operations down. As we'll see, the purpose is to keep them running smoothly.)

Once you understand the concept represented by the square, you can be as creative as you wish in creating your own kanban signals. Here are some examples:

- Cards. Attached to product as it is made and then removed and sent back as product is consumed.
- Storage Containers. When I send an empty container back to you, that is your permission to refill.
- Tanks. An upper maximum and lower minimum tank level can signal if/when to add more.
- Shipping Labels. When I open up a pallet you sent me, I can fax a copy of that label back to you as a signal.
- Kanban signals can also be electronic (as long as the floor understands and has ownership for that signal).

Your assignment here is to think of your own simple, visual, shop floor permission signal.

Kanban Pull in the Process Industry

The concept of Pull, JIT, Toyota System swept the automobile industry first, then the parts suppliers to the auto industry, and then the entire discrete manufacturing world. The reasons for its acceptance was its simplicity, its power, and the impact it had on cost, quality, inventory, and customer service—*simultaneously.*

Why, then, have we not seen it sweep through the process industry as well? Two reasons: the "We're Different" syndrome (discussed earlier) and some practical problems with applying the concepts in our environment.

The We're Different syndrome stems from the contrast between some of the classical features of a JIT (just-in-time) approach in a discrete manufacturing operation and the realities of a process plant (see Box 15.2). The practical problems of applying Pull in our process environment go back to your definition of *process*. Please go back to Section 1 for a complete discussion, but you'll remember that discrete operations converge from many (thousands?) of parts to one assembled final product. In contrast, process operations diverge from few common raw materials into many (hundreds or thousands) of final product variations.

Consider the classic Pull tool of the kanban square. In discrete parts, a station may have many upstream supply kanbans, but one downstream output kanban. If I am assembling carburetors, I may have many upstream kanbans for component parts, but as I look downstream I will see only the kanban for finished carburetors. In that environment, control is simple; the one output kanban tells us all we need to know.

In a process environment, however, we can look downstream at many (hundreds?) of kanban controls. How do we figure that out?

Box 15.2 "We're Different" JIT Features vs. Process Reality

- Cell Manufacturing. "Our process plants have large, fixed, general purpose equipment. Rearrangement into cells doesn't apply."
- Operator Line Stop. "Starting/stopping process operations are very difficult and time-consuming (certainly hours and sometimes days), so the concept of stopping operations to fix problems doesn't make sense."
- Lots of One Unit. "Our transitions are very difficult and start-up quality is very unpredictable, so small or single-unit production lots are not possible."
- "Besides, we're continuous already, so what's the big deal?"

Which square dictates? It is this problem of divergence that has always stumped us and has convinced us that, in fact, *we're different*; we are free from worrying about these ideas because they don't apply to us.

Well, we now know that is wrong. You just have to think a little creatively about how to adapt the concepts to your special circumstances. And that thinking has been done for you!

CHAPTER 16

Pull Adaptations for the Process Environment

Now that we understand the basics, I'm going to give you five special adaptation concepts; I'll bet you can come up with your own as well. Later chapters will cover design details; this chapter will introduce:

- Takt Rate
- Bottleneck Control
- Produce-To-Order (PTO) Point
- Functional Kanbans
- Product Wheels

Takt Rate

As discussed previously, *takt* is a German work that translates to "beat of the music." It is the pace at which we expect the operation to run. In the spirit of balanced production, it is the pace that we expect *all* stations to run.

Notice that I am not saying "balanced capacity" or "equal capacity." That is neither possible nor desirable. We want all stations to produce in harmony to the whole. That means that we set a Takt Rate for the end-of-the-line output and then link all stations to that Takt Rate. Somewhere in the supply chain, the bottleneck (see the next section, "Bottleneck Control") will be straining to meet takt, and all other stations will be holding back to balance with the bottleneck.

Takt Rate exiting the plant is usually set by the business team. In the presence of an MRP system (see Chapter 18), the MRP procedures will provide the Takt Rate. Overall or exit Takt Rate is not going to be constantly reset; frequency will relate to the planning period—if plans are revised once per month, that will be when takt is revisited. I can't imagine resetting exit Takt Rate more frequently than once per week, and less frequently than once per month would also be unlikely.

Within the manufacturing process, individual workstations might reset Takt Rate frequently. With nothing out of the ordinary, workstation Takt Rate is identical to exit Takt Rate. But if I am an internal supplier to you, and I know that you're going to be down for maintenance all day tomorrow, and if the intervening kanban is fairly full, I may want to rethink my immediate Takt Rate objective and slow down.

The usual process is that exit Takt Rate is fixed by the business team over the next planning period. A *much* shorter planning period is then set for each station; that might be a day, a shift, a four-hour interval. Stations communicate their expectation over that period and internal Takt Rates are adjusted accordingly. If the overall Takt Rate is 10,000 lb./hr., but I know that you are going to be down for the next eight hours and there is only 40,000 lb. of space in the kanban between us, I will readjust my immediate Takt Rate to 5,000 lb./hr. (Note: This may be an unnecessary sophistication in your system. In a well-designed system, as that kanban starts to approach full, alarms should force a decision to slow down anyway.)

Bottleneck Control

This is very much a special-case Pull adaptation. I've talked earlier about every operation having a definitive singular bottleneck. That step is the one operating at the highest percent capacity utilization, the one step that is "closest to the peg." In the case where the plant is sold out completely, the bottleneck step is operating at 100% capacity utilization, all it can do. In that sold-out case, by definition the bottleneck determines and limits the output of the entire system. Hence, if you control by the bottleneck, you control the system.

Consider an operation that consists of three steps with intervening work-in-process (WIP) inventory, drawing from a raw material stock and feeding to a Finished Product Warehouse (Figure 16.1). The middle step is the bottleneck and the system is sold out. (Remember our symbology convention: circles represent operations, triangles represent storage or inventory piles.)

In this situation, sales amounts are determined by the output of the bottleneck. Steps downstream of the bottleneck have excess capacity and can only work on material that gets through the bottleneck. Before the bottleneck, steps have excess capacity and need do no more than the bottleneck needs. To be sure that the bottleneck runs, the WIP pile before the bottleneck needs to be big enough to ensure that all surprises and variability are taken care of so that there is always material for the

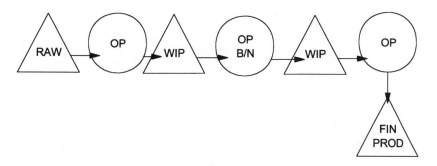

Figure 16.1   A Bottlenecked Process

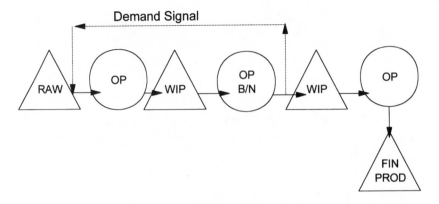

Figure 16.2 Input Linked to the Bottleneck

bottleneck to work on. (Loss of bottleneck capacity is loss of capacity for the system!) Below the bottleneck, no safety inventory is needed.

This control system, a special case of Pull, can be very simple. We need to place enough just-in-case inventory before the bottleneck. Then we need to link output from the bottleneck to the injection of new raw material into the system (see Figure 16.2). If raw material input is always equal to bottleneck output, the protective pile stays constant, the bottleneck always runs, and output of the total system is as good as it can be. The key to this approach is the demand signal that links bottleneck output to raw input; that link controls the entire system—easily, simply, visually, on the shop floor, operator owned.

Produce-To-Order (PTO) Point

This is a good example of how thinking about cycle time and attempting to apply concepts of Pull can cause one to rethink some basic paradigms and effect major gains through simple changes in approach.

The conventional BAU thinking is that customers are supplied from finished product inventory and that the manufacturing process pushes to refill the warehouse (see Figure 16.3). Time thinking recog-

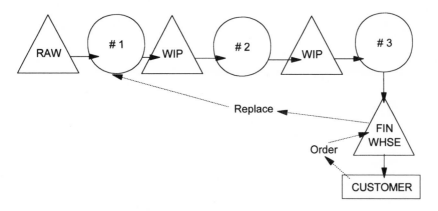

Figure 16.3 BAU Order Flow

nizes that the preceding is not necessarily so and looks at how early in the process the order can be entered. This means comparing customer order Lead Time (the quoted interval between receipt of an order and the promise to ship that order) and Cycle Time, working back from the warehouse through the process.

Let's assume that the order Lead Time is seven days, that all stations have fixed product sequences, and that Cycle Time maximum for each step in the supply chain is:

Raw Material:	5 days
Step 1 (and downstream WIP):	3 days
Step 2 (and downstream WIP):	5 days
Step 3 (not including warehouse):	1 day
Warehouse:	5 days

(This last one is obviously an arbitrary policy.)

Note that in the example in Figure 16.4, we can enter orders at Step 1 WIP inventory (literally attach the order to stock in that inventory) and move that material through Steps 2 and 3 successfully before the order is due to ship. Hence, the PTO point is just before Step 2, Steps 2 and 3 will run in response to customer order, Step 1 will run in response to its downstream WIP (its kanban), inventory downstream of Step 2 will only be material attached to a customer order on its direct

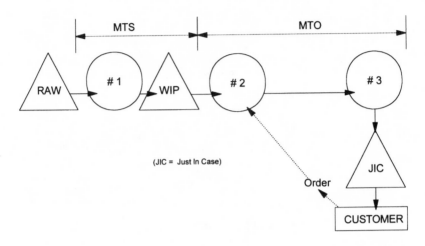

Figure 16.4   Using Produce To Order Point

way toward shipping, and the only other inventory needed is some just-in-case (JIC) inventory in the collapsed warehouse to protect key customers against unexpected outages of Steps 2 and 3.

We've accomplished all the objectives of Time and Pull: Each station is running in response to demand, inventory and Cycle Time are minimized, and all that was accomplished only by a different way of looking at the scheduling problem and the supply chain.

This is a clear illustration of what is often a point of confusion: Push/Pull versus Make-To-Stock (MTS) and Make-To-Order (MTO). Some people confuse the two sets of terms as being interchangeable, thinking that MTO equates to Pull while MTS relates to Push. That is not so: MTS resides *before* the PTO point, while MTO resides *after* the PTO point. In this example, Step 1 is MTS while Steps 2 and 3 are MTO, and both run under the concept of Pull—running in response to customer demand.

Functional Kanbans

This is nothing more than a single kanban that accepts multiple products (see Figure 16.5). The kanban is a specific size; space left in the

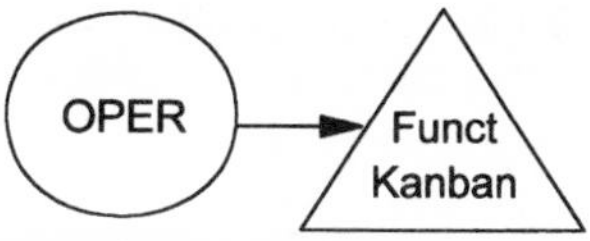

Figure 16.5 Functional Kanban

kanban gives permission to produce, and no space requires that production must stop. In a simple system with few products, this system will work well, given a little thought and inspection. "Well, there is space, but there are a lot of A's and a lot of B's . . . I guess I should make some C's."

In more complex systems, you can't rely on people interpreting functional kanbans. The additional tool that often works is a product wheel.

Product Wheels

This is another example of a concept that has been around a long time but can look dramatically different from the cycle time viewpoint. The basic idea of a product wheel is that you want to make specific products, in planned quantities, in a fixed order, and when you have finished the sequence you will loop back through the sequence again and again (see Figure 16.6).

Product wheels always show up where there is an operational need to run products in a specific order: lightest color to darkest color, heaviest unit weight to lightest, thin viscosity toward thick, and so on. However, the concept of wheels can simplify the scheduling problem even when there is not a functional need to run in a given order.

Through my career, when I was a conventional BAU manager, I had the classical approach to product wheel construction and management (see Box 16.1). At the same time, I was demanding better forecasts, not recognizing that I was contributing to a paradox (see Box 16.2). Once the nature of the paradox was realized, the question became "How short?"

☐ REGULAR SEQUENCE OF PRODUCTS
☐ IN STANDARD PLANNED QUANTITIES

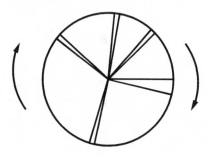

Figure 16.6   Product Wheels

Box 16.1   The BAU Product Wheel

"Give me long runs (as long as possible) so that I minimize the impact of transitions, maximize capacity, minimize cost per unit, and isolate myself from the turmoil of the marketplace."

Box 16.2   The Manufacturing
vs. Forecast Paradox

- "I desire long runs for maximum efficiency."
  But ...
- Long runs means long Cycle Time.
  And ...
- Long Cycle Time means we must forecast farther out.
  So ...
- Long runs means less accurate forecasts.
  Conclusion ...
- The prime way to improve forecasts is to reduce Cycle Time. A key way to do that is to make *shorter* runs.

Evolution of the Time Product Wheel

This is the key concept in this book. You should understand the principle and its derivation clearly.

I had always thought of a unit running on a product wheel as having capacity somewhere in excess of demand, and that we would run the unit as efficiently as we could and shut it down when we had a lull in orders.

When I began thinking about product wheels in light of Cycle Time and Pull, I was drawn to the principle that we were attempting to reduce Cycle Time and drive out waste, and that excess production generated excess waste activities. It followed that I had to match production to demand and that the way to do that was through setting correct campaign lengths of individual products and/or the time to move through the full wheel schedule. We called this "Wheel Time (Wt)" and began to consider what that Wt should be. Here is how that evolved.

The basic fundamental is that:

Over the Wt interval ...

Production = Sales (No excess production or waste)

Production = (Time in production) · (CAP)
= (Wt(1 − OUT) − ΣT) CAP

Sales = DEM (Wt)

Where: OUT = % equipment unavailability
DEM = Sales demand per unit of time
CAP = Net production capacity per unit of time when the unit is up and running
ΣT = Sum of transition times throughout one revolution of the wheel

This simplifies to:

$$Wt = \Sigma T/(I - OUT - DEM \div CAP)$$

The formula can be expanded by equating capacity to the through-put rate and net downstream yield.

$$CAP = THRU \cdot YLD$$

Where: THRU = The rate material moves through the unit when it is up and running.

YLD = Yield through the process to the point where DEM is measured. (DEM may be either final sales rate or demand for material at the next station. Be sure to set DEM and YLD on the same basis.)

The final formula then becomes:

$$Wt = \Sigma T/(I - OUT - (DEM/(THRU \cdot YLD)))$$

An example: Assume we are dealing with an extruder being used to blend fillers into a polymeric resin. The basic data is:

# of Products: 10
Transition Times: 1 hour per product plus 1 day at the end of the wheel to clean out.
OUT: 20% due to both mechanical downtime and to operator unavailability.
DEM: 15,000 lbs per day. (Average over the 10 products)
THRU: 1,000 lb. per hour when up and running
YLD: 80%

From the formula:

$$Wt = 33 \text{ hr.}/(I - 0.2 - (I5 / (24 \cdot 0.8))$$

$$= 33 \text{ hr.}/(1 - 0.2 - 0.78)$$
$$= 33 \text{ hr.}/(.02)$$
$$= 1,650 \text{ hr. or } 68.75 \text{ days}$$

Let's play a little "what if" game. Suppose your technical force does a great SPC job and cuts yield loss in half? What happens?

Check it with the Wt formula:

$$\text{Wt} = 33 \text{ hr.}/(1 - 0.2 - (15/(24 \cdot 0.9))$$
$$= 33 \text{ hr.}/(1 - 0.2 - 0.694)$$
$$= 12.97 \text{ days}$$

What's happened here? Obviously, we've gained capacity by cutting yield loss. But we achieved an 81% reduction in Wt for 10% in yield?! Apparently, the relationship between Wt and capacity may be more important than might be immediately obvious.

Wt and Capacity

When I first developed this formula, I was discussing the problem with my friend/associate Paul Veenema. When I showed him the Wt formula, he took it away to play with, and later brought back the curve shown in Figure 16.7. The superficial message of this curve is that Wt goes up as sales increase, but that the relationship is not linear, it is asymptotic to 100% utilization, and that at high utilization, the curve gets *very steep*.

The underlying "Ah Ha" is that, when you are on the steep portion of the curve, a slight change in either sales or effective current capacity produces a *huge* change in needed Wt. In contrast, if you are back on the relatively flat portion, very large changes in capacity/demand have little influence on the machine schedule. On the flat of the curve, you are bulletproof to surprises, while on the steep portion

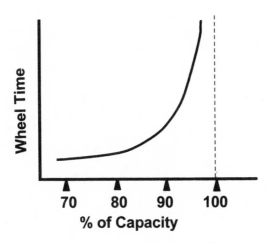

Figure 16.7 Wt vs. Capacity

you are unstable and vulnerable to any deviation. When that deviation occurs, you cannot catch up until you catch a lucky break in the other direction (see Box 16.3). This is why, in our sample Wt calculation earlier, we got such a huge Wt reduction when we cut yield loss. We were living way out at the end of the Wt curve (98% utilization), so a slight change had tremendous leverage on Wt. I'll bet many of you are in the same position: unstable but in a position to make major improvements.

Box 16.3 Wt and Capacity Management

- Management desires high/maximum capacity utilization.
- High capacity utilization ensures that the system will be *unstable*.

Some Special Wt Formula Considerations

It may help your understanding of the Wt formula to think of the denominator as *residual capacity*, capacity not consumed by production or by outage. If the denominator is equal to 0.10, there is 10% residual capacity available for transitions. If transitions require 3 days throughout one wheel revolution, it follows that the full wheel must turn in 30 days.

Some of you may notice that the denominator can go negative, that (OUT + DEM/CAP) can be greater than one. Therefore, the resultant Wt is negative. Does that mean the formula is wrong? No, it means that the situation is impossible, that the clock must literally *turn backward* to meet demand. Now, here is where it gets *really* interesting!

Wt and Inventory

We have now literally defined the amount of inventory downstream of this extruder to ensure meeting demand of the customer or the next station. For the moment, we'll ignore the problems of variation and the safety stock that requires. Assume a perfect world and the following:

- As we make each of the products, we will have to make 68.75 days supply.
- Therefore, on average at any point in time, inventory of each product will be 68.75 ÷ 2 = 34.38 days supply.
- Therefore, the downstream functional kanban fed by this wheel will have a total capacity of 34.38 · 15,000 = 515,700 lb.

Note what we've done here. We've linked the concepts of a functional kanban with a product wheel to produce a very effective Pull System

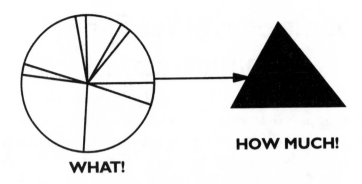

HOW MUCH!

WHAT!

Figure 16.8   Wheels and Kanbans

tool (see Figure 16.8). The wheel turns to describe the normal production schedule, but deviations in the kanban state *force* management decisions.

- Low sales cause the functional kanban to fill up. As the kanban approaches a maximum, that can be used as a signal to speed up the wheel, to respond to the inventory/capacity condition by making shorter runs and moving material faster through the system.
- High sales (or poor production) cause the kanban to drift toward a low level. That would be a signal to increase capacity by slowing the wheel, extending runs.

What we are doing is automatically matching Wt to the real-time sales/production dynamic.

A more complex and sophisticated system would involve a product wheel feeding a multiple set of kanbans, one for each product within that wheel. In that case, an instance of low sales would result in an individual product kanban reaching a maximum early, which in turn would automatically kick the wheel over into the next product segment, automatically speeding the wheel by shortening runs. The converse of high sales would give permission for longer runs by virtue of available space in the depleted kanban. In either the functional or the multiple kanban example, what we are talking about is a simple and almost automatic method for trimming the speed of the wheel by virtue of the real-world experience.

Wheel Applicability

Boxes 16.4 and 16.5 list examples of where wheels do and do not apply.

Box 16.4   Where Do Wheels Apply?

- At divergence points
- Where order flow is fairly smooth and predictable
- Where product variations must be made in a controlled sequence (colors, weights, thicknesses, etc.)
- Where capacity is constrained and schedules must be carefully managed

---

Box 16.5   Where Do Wheels Not Apply?

The inverse of the preceding box:

- Where capacity is easily available
- Where flexibility exists
- Where divergence is lacking
- Where order flow is highly erratic

CHAPTER 17

Designing
Pull Systems

You have now been given some very simple yet very powerful tools: use of the bottleneck, shifting order entry to the PTO point, and use of wheels and kanbans. Every Pull System is different and individual, adapted to the particular characteristics of the manufacturing environment. But there are always some common characteristics, as shown in Box 17.1.

Box 17.1   Pull Systems Attributes

- ■ Structured Inventory
- ■ Visible Demand Signals
- ■ Management Alarms

Structured Inventory

This means that each segment of inventory has been consciously placed into the manufacturing process, and its size or limits have been precisely defined. The questions to ask in designing inventory are:

1. Where is the PTO point? Downstream of the PTO point, all material is associated with a hard order. Inventory will consist only of work-in-process associated with filling current due orders, plus protective inventory at two possible points: the last point at which we service the customer, and behind the system bottleneck.
2. Where is the bottleneck? If the bottleneck limits sales (if we are sold out), then the bottleneck *must* be protected with inventory.
3. Which (if any) stations will operate on a wheel? If a station does operate on a wheel, there will of necessity be a downstream kanban to assure supply of all wheel products to the next station. That kanban will consist of cycle stock and safety stock.

CYCLE STOCK

The amount of cycle stock for an individual product will be the sales rate per day times the number of days between product runs, or the Wt minus this product's campaign length. If you are intending to use only one functional kanban, then the average product in that kanban at any time will have half its cycle stock remaining, so the size of the overall functional kanban will be one-half the production made during one revolution of the wheel.

If you have elected to provide multiple kanbans, one for each product in the wheel, the reasoning is the same. Each kanban must be sized to accommodate the full output of the campaign, but over time, each kanban will on average be half-full.

Safety Stock

Safety stock is to absorb variability as it occurs and is approximated by the following formula:

Safety Stock $= Z\sqrt{\sigma^2_D R^2 + \sigma^2_R D^2}$

Where:

R = Replenishment time
D = Sales demand rate
σR = Standard deviation in replenishment time
σD = Standard deviation in sales rate
Z = Service rate coefficient (coefficient of risk)

This formula assumes no Lead Time: that the product must be delivered on demand. If that is not your case, Lead Time may be factored into the formula.

Replenishment time is the *average* elapsed time from stock-out to the next production campaign. Without Lead Time, R would be one-half of Wt minus campaign length (assuming that, on average, you'll run out halfway, through the time period you are attempting to bridge). With Lead Time, R would be reduced by the Lead Time available.

Z is a recognition of the on-time performance desired. The range of options is shown in Box 17.2. (For the statisticians, you'll recognize that this assumes that sales and replenishment variation is described by a normal distribution. Z deals with covering area under a normal distribution curve. At the extremes of the curve, a much larger shift along the X axis is required to cover the same percent area. Z is, in fact, the familiar $+/-3$ sigma $= 99.7\%$ feature in Six Sigma programs.)

This formula applies whether you are designing safety stock for a single functional kanban or for multiple product kanbans.

Don't be put off or intimidated by the need to develop variability information for demand and/or replenishment time. Since we are going to build a system that literally retunes itself, all we need is a good esti-

Box 17.2

% On-Time Goal	Z Factor
84	1.0
85	1.04
90	1.28
95	1.65
97	1.88
99	2.33
99.7	3.09

mate at this point. One way to do that is to assume that we are dealing with a normal distribution and work with the fact that, in a normal distribution, more than 99% of the population is represented by a six sigma range. If I say that sales averages 10T/day, I might also estimate that the range of variation in daily sales is never less than 2T/day and never more than 20T/day. Therefore, $\sigma = (20 - 2)/6 = 3T/day$. That's all you need at this point: to get inside the ballpark; you don't have to tag second base.

THREE VARIABLES, TWO DEGREES OF FREEDOM

The safety stock formula, and the fact that it includes a service objective and a Lead Time consideration, introduces the general idea that designing inventory is a matter of making choices and trade-offs. In designing inventory, there are three variables but only two degrees of freedom. You may set any two by arbitrary policy, but the third must then float to current capability (see Figure 17.1).

For example, given a current capability, if the competitive situation dictates a certain Lead Time and a specific On-Time performance against that Lead Time, then you must accept the inventory level that is required. If you decide that you must limit inventory and you have a

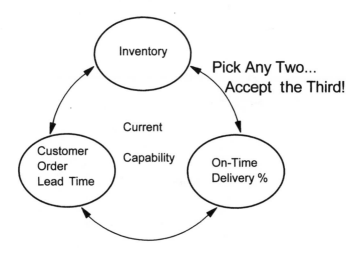

Figure 17.1 Three Variables, Two Degrees of Freedom

firm Lead Time policy, then you must accept the On-Time performance that will result. After coming to grips with what the current reality must be, you can then set out to improve your future-state capability and to take advantage of that improvement in one of those three parameters.

A Design Example

As we talk about these principles of design, I'll illustrate with a real-life example: a Vermont paperboard company. A basic flowchart of their process is shown in Figure 17.2. The critical factors in this company's performance were:

- A four-week customer order Lead Time.
- 65% On-Time delivery performance.
- 10% board machine mechanical downtime.
- High (95%) board machine capacity utilization.
- 15% yield-loss downstream of the board machine.

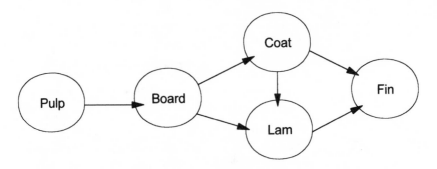

Figure 17.2 A Paperboard Process

- A Cycle Time (inventory in terms of days of supply) in excess of 60 days.
- A general knowledge that there was more market available, *if* they could find the capacity to service that market, and *if* they could provide better service to attract that market.
- A general recognition that the board machine was the bottleneck, *but*...

  A practice of focusing on the finishing steps to expedite due orders, leading to...

  A tendency to jerk the board machine around.
- A practice of attempting to run all 80 paper grades on the board machine in about a six-week production cycle.
- A recognition that it required about five days to move material through the operations downstream of the board machine.

Given that environment, management was concerned with finding means to gain capacity, reduce inventories, and/or provide better service.

Our initial analysis dealt with the fact that we had to give recognition to the board machine and to develop better discipline around the management of that bottleneck. A Wt for a simple 80-product board machine wheel showed that 83 days would be required. That clarified why the plant ran in a chaos mode and why delivery performance was so poor; they were trying to follow a production cycle that was almost exactly half of that required! No wonder they were continually scrambling.

Using Wt Analysis as an Improvement Planning Tool

When we began working with this company, management had recognized their inventory/capacity issues and had formed three independent teams: Transitions, Maintenance, and Yield. To gauge the impact potential, we asked each team to estimate the improvement they might expect to make in their parameter and plugged each improvement independently into the Wt formula. The potential for each team was:

- Maintenance—6-day reduction in Wt
- Transitions—7-day impact
- Yield—67-day Wt reduction!!!

Here is a living example of life on the steep portion of the Wt curve. This company was living at 95% capacity utilization and was very unstable, but it had a major opportunity to move down the curve and gain tremendous improvements.

Further, what is the chance that one team will have a negative impact on another? If we are trying to get back on production quicker after a production change, what is the chance that we will add to yield loss? If we are trying to keep equipment up and running, or get a machine back quicker after a failure, what is the probability of hurting yield? Obviously, both the Yield and Maintenance teams had little chance to improve Wt, and significant chance to hurt Yield. We quickly disbanded both teams and focused on our major opportunity—yield.

Complex Wheel Design

Going to an 83-day wheel was certainly not in the final best interests of this company. The inventory required to bridge 83-day intervals between production campaigns of all 80 products was staggering. Obviously, we needed a more creative and satisfactory solution.

One of the best ways of reducing Wt is the reduction of transition times. Since ΣT is the numerator, a reduction in transitions is directly translatable to a reduction in Wt: X% reduction in one produces an identical X% reduction in the other. One approach to ΣT is to do the SMED work of reducing transition times, the other is to (artificially) reduce the number of transitions contained in the wheel. This can be done by building more complex wheel structures.

In the case of this company, they paretoized their product line and created three product groupings:

- A Products: high-volume strategic
- B Products: midvolume but strategic
- C Products: low-volume maintenance

With that distinction, they then built three wheels (see Figure 17.3). In this design, all A's appear in each wheel, B's are spread across all three wheels, and some C's appear in Wheel 3. In the case of C's, customers are contacted as we approach Wheel 3, needs are determined, and about one-third of the C's are run in each Wheel 3, running enough to provide needs to cover the next two three-wheel sequences.

As each of these wheels has a limited number of products, ΣT for each wheel is much less than for the 80-product wheel and Wt is also proportionally less. With some supporting improvements in transition times and in yields, these three wheels calculated to wheel times of about 20 days each.

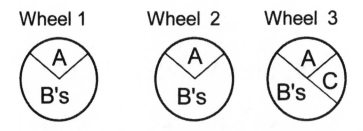

Figure 17.3 Complex Wheel Design

That produced a very interesting benefit: Since A's carried a 30-day Lead Time and were produced every 20 days, they could be produced to customer order instead of to inventory! Similarly, since we solicited customer need for C's at the start of Wheel 3, we could produce for 180-day need for those products that were to be included in that particular wheel. Hence, C's also were to be produced to order. Only B's, which were to be produced every 60 days against a 30-day Lead Time needed to be produced to a maintained inventory.

Notice what this does: It positions different categories of products on different portions of the Wt curve (see Figure 17.4). By putting A's into a position where they are produced within customer Lead Time and to customer order, A's have been made very stable and predictable. Similarly, B's have been improved by virtue of being able to build planned inventories. Granted, C's have been put out at the extreme end of the curve, but you have a chance every 60 days to review the bidding on individual products that you have planned to be able to make only every 180 days.

Last, since we now knew that we had to build B inventory to bridge 60-day intervals, we were in a position to very precisely define the

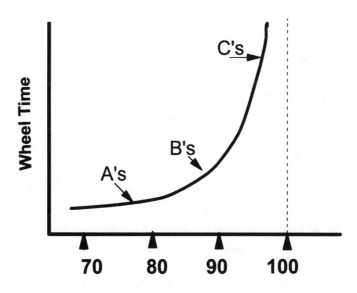

Figure 17.4   Positioning Products on the Wt Curve

structure of the B inventory: both cycle stock and just-in-case safety stock inventory.

This leads to consideration of the second characteristic of Pull Systems, creating visible demand.

Creating Visible Demand

The general principle here is that we want each station to see concrete evidence of its downstream customer's need: If the customer is about to run out, I want to panic; if they are not taking for some reason, I want to slow up accordingly.

In the trivial case where stations are side-by-side, visible demand is easy; you can see the kanban square. In cases where visibility is not direct, you are limited only by your imagination. Some examples include:

- Cards can be attached to each production unit and sent back to the producing station when the material is used.
- The transportation container—box, tank, pallet, and so on—can be sent back when empty.
- A variation of the container for the film or paper industry can be the roll core, returned to be rewound with product when it is empty.
- Product labels can be faxed from thousands of miles away from customer to supplier as the containers are moved into production.

Demand signals can also be electronic, such as material inventories on a display screen. But I view that as a last resort because it does not have the involvement, connection, the intimacy of a visual signal. People are less likely to understand and to trust a computer-generated signal.

In the case of the paper company example, we chose to use cards. Steps in setting up and activating that system were straightforward:

1. Since we had calculated the Wt, the campaign length for each product, and the safety stock required, we knew the size of the

kanban for each product (the amount of material that would be in inventory immediately after each campaign was completed).

2. We put up an array of card racks by the board machine—a set of racks for each of the three wheels, one individual rack for each B product. The racks themselves were arranged from left to right in the same order that products were positioned in the three-wheel structure. (Picture a time-card rack.)

3. We issued plastic laminated roll cards for each B product. The number of cards issued was equivalent to a completely full kanban for every product.

4. We then went through the inventory and tagged all existing rolls. In many cases, there were more rolls in inventory than there were cards. Necessarily, we left those rolls untagged and attempted to use those rolls first. Where we had extra cards, they went in the card rack as evidence that there was demand for that product.

The result was an array of card racks, one for each product in the three wheels, arranged in left-to-right order matching the planned production sequence. Each rack is similar to a bar graph; the full height indicates the size of the kanban. Within each rack, empty slots indicate that rolls are in the kanban while cards indicate demand for production into the kanban. The system was completed by adding some bells and whistles for the purpose of alerting management.

Management Alarms

Whatever your demand display system, you'll want to be alerted if the system is drifting off from plan. Drift includes demand above expectation and/or production shortfalls. In other words, the kanban might fill up because of either lack of sales or excess production. Kanbans might go empty because of either sales booms or production losses. You want to know and react before you get into an extreme position.

In the paper company case, the team came up with some very creative alarm signals:

- *Kanban Alarms*. When a product campaign completes, and the kanban for that product is full, the card rack is empty. You expect that rack to slowly refill as other products are being made, reaching full just as you come back to that product on the wheel. Therefore, we needed to be alerted if the rack was refilling too fast, if there was danger of running out before we returned. To do that, we color-coded each wheel: red, blue, and green. We could then identify a specific card slot for each product that should coincide with completing each wheel. If we have just completed product X in the red wheel, we know the last slot that should remain empty when we finish the red, the blue, and the green wheel. If that slot gets filled before the wheel completes, we are either refilling the racks (consuming product) faster than expected or the wheels are behind schedule. Either way, there is a danger that we will run out.

  The specific mechanism for this was to use colored tape stripes, such that if there is a card in that slot, the tape stripe is covered and can't be seen. With no card in the slot, the color stripe is visible.

  In the general case, then, I should be able to quickly scan the card racks and see every alarm slot corresponding in color to the wheel now running. "I'm in the middle of the red wheel, and for Product Y over in the green wheel the red slot is covered. Product Y is in alarm state."

  The kanban alarms were reported every morning. Question: Are alarms OK? Answer: It depends. You don't want to *never* have alarms; the system would be too fat. But the more alarms on, the more likely you'll actually have a stock-out. Once the paper company system settled down, two to three alarms for 35 kanbans was normal.

- *Wheel Position*. We expected the three example wheels to turn in 20 days each. It was important for decision making to know where actual wheel position was at any time. The team's solution to this was very clever. Since the racks were arranged in production order from left to right, two racecar icons—one for Plan and one for Actual—were put above the rack display and moved every day to show the current state.

- *System Discipline*. BAU attitudes are hard to kill; people will always want to extend a run that is going well, to "dump" a transition over onto the next shift, and so on. The team wanted ways to make this type of behavior obvious. The result was that they set up two special kanbans.

- *Overrun Stock.* Because there is a significant time lag between batch pulp makeup and the board machine, it is difficult to exactly time the end of the run. Recognizing that, the team set up a small kanban of overrun cards. If workers ran out of kanban cards before a run completed, they could use the overrun card(s). The procedure then called for retagging the overrun roll with a proper product card as soon as one was returned from downstream. If manufacturing used *all* the overrun cards, that was discussed in morning meeting, looking for *why* they had abused the system.

- *Held Stock.* In some cases, quality of a particular roll is in question when it is first made and put into inventory. In the old environment, there was no reason to push for final disposition, and inventory got clogged with material held up for quality disposition. Here again, a small Held kanban was established and rolls tagged accordingly when a full release could not be made. If the supply of Held cards ran out, the only way to get more was to release something currently held. Morning meeting discussions on this issue became very brief.

These alarm conditions are discussed at every shift change and in the morning production meeting. Even if stock-outs do not ultimately occur, alarms enter into decisions. Questions concerning maintenance priority, schedule changes, customer special requests, Lead Time adjustments all become almost self-evident when you relate them to the kanban/wheel conditions.

Result: Paper Company Example

In this example, more things were done than simply installing a Pull System. Work was done on yields, transition capability, the product line was reviewed, order policies questioned and revised, and so on. But the Pull System *was* a major contributor in the following ways:

- Inventory was reduced 66%. Cycle Time went from 60 days to 20 days.
- Lead Time was reduced from four weeks to two weeks.
- On-time performance went from 65% to 95%.
- No kanban has actually gone empty. (This says there is still room for Cycle Time improvement.)
- Capacity gains through yield and through bottleneck management were significant. (Process changes were made at the same time and relative impact can't be separated, but estimates would be at least 10% in capacity through management/policy changes.)

CHAPTER 18

Additional Design and Management Considerations

Handling Demand Variations

Under normal operation, the wheel is almost self-managing or self-correcting. If/when demand drops off, kanbans will empty more slowly, they will be partially full when the wheel "arrives" at them, runs will be shorter as kanbans require less time to refill, and the wheel will *automatically* turn faster (as it should). Conversely, if demand picks up, kanban safety stock will be reduced, kanbans will be closer to empty when it comes time to refill, runs will be longer, and the wheel time will extend. Essentially, one slides up and down the wheel time curve in response to varying demand (see Figure 18.1).

There is, however, a very critical special case that occurs when average demand is near capacity. If average or design demand is, for example, 95% of maximum, no problem is posed by a minimum demand of 83% (see Figure 18.2). In that situation the wheel would speed up in response in order to maintain inventory and Cycle Time. But overall capacity is consumed when that happens. If the maximum demand is near or above 100%, the system will not be able to respond

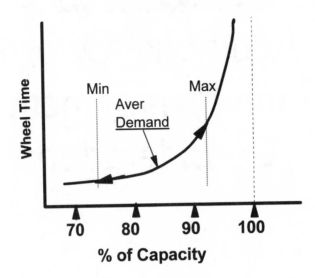

Figure 18.1   Shifting on the Wt Curve as Demand Changes

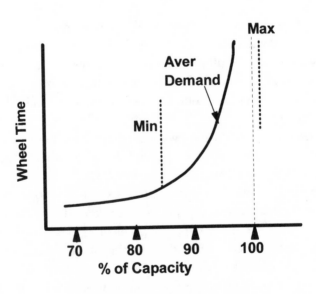

Figure 18.2   An Impossible Case

to that when it happens. Conclusion: When maximum expected demand exceeds capacity, the system cannot be allowed to consume capacity during periods of soft demand.

I would first maintain that this represents poor capacity management, that one should manage capacity expansions to avoid this situation. But here are the necessary adaptations for this situation:

1. Fix the wheel speed at average demand.
2. Identify high-volume stable products that can be inventoried to absorb swings.
3. Establish strategic kanbans that will be opened and filled when demand falls below average.
4. Utilize these kanbans to augment capacity when demand exceeds the average.

The net effect is that the wheel always turns at average demand, and strategic kanbans are used to occupy capacity when demand is soft and to support sales when demand is high.

Dealing with Straight-Through Operations

We've talked extensively about wheels, but I don't want to overemphasize them. Wheels are a great tool where they have applicability, but they aren't universal. (The previous chapter included a checklist for applicability.)

In the previous section, under the subject of modeling, we showed an example of a catalyst operation (see Figure 11.2). That operation is characterized by extremely "lumpy" order receipt; it only gets about 20 "events" per year. And the plant has about 20 different product variations and all take different routes through that operation (they don't all start in at the same point, many loop back several times, some exit at different points, etc.) It's like maintaining a food plaza subject to the infrequent and random arrival of huge and very hungry grizzly bears who take random walks through the plaza. If you run out of food, they'll eat you!

The catalyst plant is an extreme example of a straight-through operation; material shows up at a station and expects to flow through that point as it arrives.

Straight-through operations are essentially queuing theory problems. The classic example, as mentioned earlier, is the bank teller problem. You operate a bank and you have to decide how to schedule the teller windows so that customers who arrive randomly are satisfied without a wasteful excess of tellers. Through a knowledge of arrival rates and teller service capacity (and variability in both), predictions can be made concerning average and maximum waiting line length, percentage of customers who will leave, and teller efficiency.

Some of you may have the statistical horsepower to answer queue questions directly. I find that these problems lend themselves well to modeling.

Capacity/Demand Considerations in Straight-Through Operations

When we discussed product wheels, we developed a curve for Wheel Time versus Percent Capacity Utilization. That showed that the system became unstable and that inventory grew geometrically as sales approached maximum capacity. *It is just the same with a straight-through operation!*

I'll give you two abstract examples. How do highway engineers make the decision about number of lanes? They know that highways can accommodate a certain density of cars. Beyond that density, traffic flow drops sharply even though there is no obstruction. A personal variation of that ... I recently left New York City via the Lincoln Tunnel. As I entered the tunnel, which is two lanes wide, a car stalled in one of the lanes. You would expect that travel time would have doubled, but because traffic was bumper-to-bumper, it took more than 10 minutes to travel what is certainly less than one mile. Material movement through a plant of given capacity behaves in exactly the same manner; as you strain the limits of capacity, flow becomes congested, service becomes unstable, and material piles up.

Managing/Maintaining the System

Since the environment is dynamic and ever-changing, a Pull System is never done. You must have the mechanism for keeping the system in tune. In the paper example, the team set up two mechanisms for keeping the system in tune:

1. The Simple system. The direct way to retune the system is to use the information the system gives you, in the form of alarms and stock-outs, to do the returning. The team set up a simple retuning process used at the end of every three-wheel cycle that follows these rules:
    *   If a kanban alarms, the alarm is desensitized by moving the color stripe down one slot. (In this design, racks are filled from top to bottom. This allows the return of one more card before the alarm goes on.)
    *   If the kanban goes empty, one card and one slot are added to the kanban.
    *   If the kanban does not go empty, one card and one slot are taken away.
2. The Formal system. A spreadsheet was developed to do the initial kanban calculations: Wt, run lengths, cycle and safety stocks,

alarm points. This spreadsheet is rerun quarterly or whenever a major product offering change occurs. With the new spreadsheet, it is relatively easy to rebuild the system by adding/removing cards and slots. Changes are *only* made if the product line has been changed or is a kanban is off by more than 20% (deviations of less than 20% are left to the Simple system).

The only other maintenance considerations are special situations, typically shutdowns or special selling opportunities.

If a shutdown is upcoming, and inventory must be built to bridge the shutdown outage, it is a simple matter to temporarily expand the kanbans, issue temporary cards (which gives additional permission to produce, which automatically causes the wheels to slow down), and then extract the extra card and to shrink the kanbans back to normal when the shutdown is over.

Occasionally, the Sales Manager may have a special (onetime) sales opportunity. He or she may not be certain of the sale, is not willing to build the added volume into the ongoing forecast, but wants to invest in the inventory. In this case, a special kanban is built, the inventory is made to fill it, but the resultant cycle time is the responsibility of the sales office, not the manufacturing group. It is held until sold, or until sales renounces the need.

A single person (or office) should be appointed as the keeper of the system to manage strategic kanbans, regular retuning, special sales or shutdown situations, and the periodic rebuilding to the system. That person usually is the person who filled the role of scheduler in the BAU environment. The person is elevated from fighting daily fires and expediting to a role of managing and administering a structure that provides information and direction to all.

A Generic Pull Design Checklist

The preceding emphasis was on designing for a process environment and on tools to manage the process industry problem of divergence. But what if you're not in that environment? What if you come from the more traditional discrete industry—screw, nut, bolt, fab and assembly? Was all of the preceding for naught? No, it wasn't; all of the same principles apply.

But, to address the general or generic case, here is a general purpose checklist of considerations for applying Pull in your special case:

1. Map the material flow. (If you're following our process, you will have done so already.) The map does not have to be at the detail level, but you need to see major equipment steps. Use the circle/triangle convention for operations and for inventory, and make them big enough that you can make notations within the symbols.

2. Identify the bottleneck step. *Don't assume that you know this answer: Do the calculation.* For each step, go through calculating the practical capacity considering the instantaneous rate less transition times, machine downtime, and material yield losses; in other words, what each unit can be expected to produce. Compare that with demand and develop a percent loaded for each unit. The unit most loaded is, by definition, the bottleneck. One variation: If you have an area or process step that contains several parallel units (casting machines in a paper mill, parallel extruders in a resin plant), and one of those units calculates to be the bottleneck, you may want to operate as though the area as a whole is the bottleneck. Mark the bottleneck on your material flow map.

3. Identify the Produce-To-Order (PTO) point. Start at the end of the process and sum Cycle Times for individual steps, working back into the process until you find the point where Cycle Time equals Lead Time. This is the point at which orders could be entered with time for them to flow through the remainder of the operation and complete before they become due. The PTO point separates upstream Make-To-Stock (MTS) and downstream Make-To-Order (MTO). Mark the PTO point on your material flow map.

4. Identify divergence points, where SKUs multiply.

5. Consider use of product wheels. Wheels will be used where products must be made in a particular sequence and/or where capacity is limited and must be managed carefully.

6. Identify critical control points. You'll probably want to control how material enters the process (by linking to the bottleneck). Insertion of orders at the PTO point effectively controls downstream operations. Bottlenecks exert control on all downstream operations.

7. Position inventory. Bottlenecks require protective inventory. Inventory will be downstream of any product wheels. Protective inventory must be held at the customer service point. Distinguish between normal cycle stock and safety stock, being careful that safety stock is not redundant; properly calculated, bottleneck and customer safety stocks are each only needed *once*.

8. Consider all straight-through operations, their capacity, and whether flows can be stable. You may want to consider modeling the operation if capacity utilization is approaching 90%.

9. Size the inventory piles using the cycle stock and safety stock formulas. Don't worry about making estimates of variation; the system itself will adjust for any error in your estimate.

10. Plan how to signal demand between stations. Think *simple, visual, common sense;* cards, containers, floor squares, and so on. Let floor people get involved.

11. Plan for management alarms. How will we know if the system is drifting off? This includes drift in production, order receipt, and/or inventory amounts. Again, think simple, visual, common sense. Include responsibility for recognizing alarms, how they get reported, and who/where action is taken.

12. Identify a person responsible for maintaining and retuning the system. Plan procedures for fine-tuning on a continuing basis and for periodic complete rebuilding of the system (perhaps quarterly, coincident with a new sales forecast?).

13. Plan to include Pull status in regular shift/area/management meetings.

14. Integrate with MRP or other formal scheduling/inventory/planning functions. Pull is the shop-floor execution and control mechanism underneath your planning process. Look back to the Management Process map in Section 3; Pull represents the control level in that map.

Isn't This in Conflict with MRP?

Often I encounter companies that have invested heavily in computer-ized scheduling systems or central scheduling organizations, or both. If the Steering Team has not done its work, if the central scheduling organization is not represented on the Steering Team, if objectives were not clearly delineated, there can be *major* conflict between the scheduling function and the idea of Pull. After all, we're talking simple, visual, shop floor, operator owned! How can that not be seen as incompatible and threatening to the central scheduling people?

The generic conflict here is between MRP and Pull. To under-stand, we need to define MRP. Classical, old, traditional MRP was nothing more than automated Push. A sales forecast was converted into area master schedules and each area then was evaluated against schedule completion. The definition of success for each area almost degraded to whether you had your downstream customer buried in product.

The central idea of traditional MRP was central, automated, com-puterized. Three basic features of classical MRP are exploded sched-ules, time phasing and sequencing. *Explosion* is taking a Bill of Materi-als for the final product, the schedule for production of that final product, and exploding back into schedules for each component. *Time phasing* refers to cascading back through the process and identifying the required procurement or production date for each raw material and component, based on the final production date for the assembly. *Sequencing* refers to the order in which job orders are going to be run at each workstation.

From our preceding work, it should be obvious that time phasing and sequencing may not apply in our process environment. Often, sta-tions *must* produce in a particular order: light to dark, thin to thick, and so on. So sequencing is often defined by the process itself. Time phas-ing implies that we can coordinate schedules of individual stations. But we've just seen that stations on wheels have a specific and rigid sched-ule that they must follow to match production to demand, to avoid the sins of excess production. How then do I coordinate with a wheel? It is unthinkable that two wheels would coordinate with each other; they will certainly turn at different speeds unless all design parameters are absolutely identical. The only other way to coordinate is to have a station that is infinitely flexible—not likely. So, in a process environment, precise coordination and time phasing are not likely.

The primary concern over MRP is that it smells like Push. In traditional MRP, schedules were fixed and stations were measured against schedule attainment. If that resulted in mismatches in pace between stations, buildup of materials, and disconnection between stations, so be it. Competition between stations (and local optimization by each station) were encouraged.

Happily, traditional MRP has evolved. There are many very positive aspects of MRP. MRP begins with Sales and Operational Planning (SOP), a very necessary feature for managing/planning the business and the overall supply chain. It provides long-range inventory, resource, and capacity planning, and it sets up accountability for performance against the plan. One of the products of the SOP process is setting Takt Rate for the plant based on the dynamics of sales, capacity, shutdown plans, seasonality, product development/test time, new product introductions, and so on.

What happens, then, when a well-structured MRP planning process runs up against a manufacturing process that is capable of flowing materials through the process in response to a needed exit rate while maintaining planned internal inventory levels and alerting management to internal deviations as they occur?

With newer MRP approaches, the SOP process is used to set takt for output from the plant, and the Bill of Materials is one level. The MRP system "thinks" that end products come straight from raw materials, and the intervening stations are left to manage themselves. (When raw materials vendors are integrated into the Pull System, they also may be invisible to MRP.) Progressive MRP designers love Pull, in that it makes the design and operation of MRP easier. All the control and accountability (to SOP) is maintained, but the detail complexity is simplified.

The distinction between the two should be clear. MRP is a very essential *planning* process. Capacity, sales, and resource needs are carefully planned by MRP; in fact, the very structure of Pull depends on the

Are We Done Yet?

- Coincident with the work required for Section 3, the Cycle Time for each portion of the manufacturing process is identified.
- The PTO point has been identified. This divides the process into a portion that will be Make-To-Stock and a portion that is Make-To-Order.
- Everyone understands that both MTS and MTO portions of the process can/will run under a Pull discipline. (MTS does *not* equate to Push.)
- The need for inventory at every point has been challenged. Inventory *is* needed to protect the customer service point, to protect the bottleneck, to maintain supply below a wheel. All other points should be severely questioned.
- Pull System has been designed. Features of the system include carefully structured inventory including both cycle and safety stocks, visible demand signals at every station, and management alarms.
- A person or office responsible for being keeper of the system is identified.
- Actions to be taken during demand peaks and valleys have been anticipated.
- The system has considered, and includes, methods for enforcing the discipline of the system (for disclosing abuse of the system).
- Management has been trained and knows how to use alarm information. An informed response to alarms is ensured.
- Pull is compatible and integrated with any central scheduling, inventory, and distribution functions.
- A system for continually reviewing and updating the Pull System is in place. This includes both regular retuning and occasional complete rebuild.
- All operations have been trained in the mechanics and the reasons for Pull.
- The system has in some way been through a dry-run shakedown.
- Around-the-clock coverage is provided for the initial run-in period.

information provided by MRP. Pull, in contrast, is a very effective *shop floor execution* tool for operating against the plan. The Management Process map suggested in Section 2 distinguishes between a planning function, a control function, and an execution function. In scheduling and inventory management, MRP is the planning engine and Pull provides the control. That degree of understanding and compatibility between MRP and Pull is only obtained by the Steering Team working hard on expectations up front.

How Will We Know When We're Done?

As with the other sections in this book, this section ends with a checklist of what needs to be accomplished in a Pull installation. As noted, this section is done in parallel with Section 3, "Planning and Assessing." When you're satisfied with your work on both, proceed to Section 5, "Visible Management and Continuous Improvement."

Visible Management and Continuous Improvement

You do not install quality; you begin to work at it.

—*W. Edwards Deming*

CHAPTER 19

Visible Management

Introduction:
Are We Done Yet?

We've done a *lot* of work together. We've organized into a Business Steering Team and a Time Core Team. We've rethought our business strategy and created focused and balanced performance metrics to guide us. We've mapped our entire process and identified waste and opportunities within that process. We may have even simulation modeled that process. We've analyzed, processed, and condensed those opportunities down into a specific action plan. We've looked over the traditional TQM tools and picked the *very few* that will have immediate major impact on our selected metrics. We've planned to implement the special Time concepts of Group Technology and Visible Management. Most important, we've built a Pull System to manage the shop floor ... by the shop floor! We've done all the necessary planning and accountability work to ensure that these new concepts go into use seamlessly and effectively. An impressive list ... aren't we done?

No, we have only positioned ourselves so that we can now do the most important segment of this journey. Up to now, all we have done is put systems in place to do the best job possible of managing the current state and our current capability level. What we will do in this last section is to use what we have put in place as a platform for putting a continuous improvement process in place so that we will continue (forever) to use what these systems tell us in order to drive our capability inexorably upward.

Specifically, we are going to be sure that we are capturing the problems that detract from shop floor perfection, that we are analyzing those detractors and condensing them into core root cause issues, and we will revise our management systems so that we effectively eliminate those core causes. In addition, we will provide a method for continually rating our capability and tracking our progress toward the perfect (but never reachable) state.

Visible Management

We broached this subject in Section 3, now we're going to finish it off completely.

A basic tenet of our continuous improvement approach is two-way communication: *up* the organization and *down* (see Box 19.1).

In BAU (Business As Usual) management (although it may not be openly recognized or expressed) the mind-set is "We know what the shop floor needs! It's our job to tell them what to do and it's their job to get it done!" In our Time approach, that is completely reversed. "They (shop floor) tell us what they need. It's our job to provide that ... or to help them provide for themselves." These shop floor needs are captured via the Visible Management tools you have provided. The basic concept is shown in Figure 19.1.

We talked about Takt Boards in Section 3; you should have designed something like the one in Figure 19.1 for each operating area or major workstation. The major questions in that design were:

Box 19.1   Continuous Improvement in Time

- Needs flow *up* from the floor.
- Resources and solutions flow *down* to the floor.

- How often do we set Takt Rate? At the end of the process, Takt Rate is being set by the business team, by the Sales and Operations meeting, by the MRP system. It is set once each planning session, for the next planning period. That period is probably a month, certainly no less than a week and not more than a quarter.

   Within the process, at each workstation, Takt Rate may be the same as the exit Takt Rate, or the local Takt Rate can be reset based on the immediate downstream conditions. If Takt Rate is to be locally reset, how frequently will we do that?

- How often will we report accomplishment against takt and capture the detracting reasons if takt has not been met? I don't want this to be too short an interval; I'll burden people with all the reporting, and I'll drown in minutiae. On the other hand, if the reporting interval is too long, I will get blurred information. For example, if I report once per day, there may be many causes for not meeting Takt

TAKT BOARDS

TIME	WHAT		WHY NOT	WHO OWNS	WHEN FIXED
	WANT	IS			

PURGED WEEKLY

Figure 19.1   A Typical Takt Board

during that interval, and I want only one reason per line on the Takt Board. That long an interval leaves a lot of room for argument about what the key event was and/or a lot of generalization. The usual reporting period falls somewhere between two hours and one work shift, depending on your own characteristics.

- How do I rationalize the work of keeping this board up-to-date with other paperwork? I don't want to write something on the board, in a paper log, and into a computer file. Part of setting up this system is to simplify other record keeping. You'll want to make a list of all paperwork currently done by the operators and test each for value-add, just as you did with the operating steps. Eliminate any redundancies and nonvalue records, so that the visual displays are as vital, and as accepted, as possible.

The first result of these Takt Boards is that you can walk through the process and, in a matter of minutes, get the pulse of the operation. Are we succeeding? If not, why not? Who's got the ball? When will it be fixed? And everyone can get that same pulse. Problems become obvious.

You'll want to consider some other features for your boards, for example, kanban state. Obviously, kanban state can have a critical influence on the operation. You'll want some way of making kanban conditions obvious, and the Takt Board may be the right place for that. Thermometer displays are one simple and effective way to do that (see

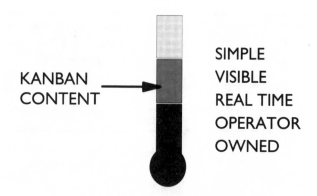

Figure 19.2   Displaying Kanban State

Metrics...

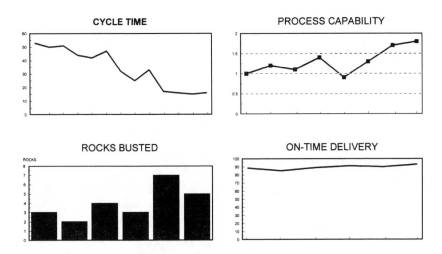

Figure 19.3 Typical Takt Board Displays

Figure 19.2). You might choose to use graphs to show trends over time, or you might use electronic/computer terminals, but I would urge you to keep these displays simple and easy to understand.

You'll also want to consider a display of key metrics (see Figure 19.3). The Takt Board should be your central communication tool, and progress against the critical performance measures is an obvious addition to the basic board.

Finally, you may think about posting to the Takt Board such things as:

- Company newsletters
- Team meeting summaries
- A listing of active "Rabbits" (key problems) and their owners
- Pictures of people who have successfully captured their rabbit

CHAPTER 20

Linking Visible Management with Continuous Improvement

Our premise is that we want continuous improvement driven by/from the shop floor; the Takt Board is the tool for doing that and the method is simple (note: I didn't say "easy"):

- Problems (failure to meet takt) are purged from the board (captured, copied down, whatever) on a regular basis.
- Problems are reduced to an underlying root cause.
- Root causes are paretoized.

You'll need to assign someone the task of capturing, doing root cause, and paretoizing. As much as possible, for the purpose of ownership, you would like this to be shop floor people. But you may have some problems with root cause and with pareto work.

Root Cause

Here we are trying to distinguish between *symptom* and *cause*. If you deal with symptoms, and don't get after cause, the symptom will keep repeating. What we are looking for here is complete and permanent elimination of the underlying cause.

In a former life, I did a good deal of work as a seminar leader in industrial safety management. One of the concepts we taught was the idea of a Correction Hierarchy (see Box 20.1). The proper thought process is to think from the bottom of the chart upward, first attempting to eliminate. That should be obvious (and I'm sure it is to you), but our experience over and over again is that even the most experienced safety pro thought from the top down. Training always seems to be quick and easy, but people forget that you must then train and retrain forever. Elimination, however, is forever. Sometimes, it is financially or practically impossible to eliminate, so, reluctantly, one must fall back on guarding. And sometimes it is financially or practically impossible to guard, so *very reluctantly* one falls all the way back on training. But the first thought should always be to eliminate.

Managing a manufacturing operation is no different than managing safety. We want to permanently eliminate problem *causes*, not just fire-fight the symptoms of them (see "A Safety Analogy" in Box 20.2).

One of the easiest and most straightforward ways of converting symptoms into causes is the "Five Why" process. The idea is that, if I ask you "Why?" a maximum of five times, I will move from the visible symptom to the underlying cause. An example is shown in Box 20.3. The important point of this is: If you try to treat the symptom, it will

---

Box 20.1   A Safety Correction Hierarchy

- Training and Procedures
- Guarding
- Elimination

Box 20.2   A Safety Analogy

In my days as a safety educator, I did extended work for the Australian mining industry and had the opportunity to spend time with miners in the outback.

The format of the seminar was to ask for example injuries that had occurred in their experience and to then analyze those injuries for their effect (often devastating), causes, and means of prevention.

One participant offered up a story of a person who was setting up a remote geology camp, including a latrine. The latrine included a roof, and when the worker completed the roof he jumped three feet down to the ground, landed wrong, and broke a leg.

I knew they had gotten the point of the hierarchy when we discussed prevention. I expected everyone to talk about training people not to jump off of roofs, but their solution was to build the roof structure on its side ... standing it upright when complete!

Box 20.3   A "Five" Why Example

- "You were late to work this morning. "Why were you late?"
  — "I overslept."
- "Why did you oversleep?"
  — "My alarm clock didn't go off."
- "Why didn't it go off?"
  — "I forgot to set it last night when I went to bed."
- "Why did you forget to set it?"
  — "I was blitzed when I came in from the party!"

Symptom: Attendance Problem
Root Cause: Substance Abuse

come back over and over again. We've all been in plants that had, somewhere in the organization, a Mr. or Ms. Fix-it, someone who was adept at putting out fires and who was repeatedly acclaimed a hero for doing so. The fact was, he or she fixed the same problems repeatedly, by treating the symptom.

The absolute classic example of a symptom treater was a scheduling supervisor who was famous for being able to give emergency service to critical customers. He did that by maintaining a secret supply of inventory, thereby withholding information from the customer service and distribution people and *creating* the very problem he would become a hero over.

Creating Cause Categories

It often helps the analysis process to create root cause categories, or bins, and to then use the Five Why process to properly place a problem in a category. Box 20.4 lists one suggested set of cause categories; you can make your own tailored version. (Note: You'll want to create your own subgroups within each category. You'll need subgroups that are specific enough that resulting logical corrective action efforts are obvious.)

The most popular of the causes listed in the box will be External because that equates to "It's not my fault! It couldn't be helped."

Box 20.4   Root Cause Subcategories

- Mechanical Failure
- Process Documentation
- Process Design
- Product Design
- Operating Disconnect
- Raw Materials
- External

Again, I want to equate this to safety management. Du Pont is *the* safest industrial company. Their lost-time injury rate is 0.03/200,000 man-hours. 200,000 hours is the OSHA reporting standard and is about what a 100-person crew would work in one year. The rate is truly amazing; that fictitious crew would work almost 30 years before suffering an injury. In fact, they have plants that have gone over 50 million man-hours, or almost 30 years, without injury. Their workers are *10 times* safer on the job than in their own homes.

Du Pont's two basic safety principles are:

1. All injuries, no matter how slight, must be reported to supervision immediately. (They don't achieve their records by playing games with the numbers.)
2. All injuries can be prevented. Key words are *all* (they don't say *some* or *most*) and *can* (they've never had a full year with absolutely zero).

The second principle is the key; another way of wording it is to say that every experience can be blocked from repeating. That means they can never say "That one was unavoidable; it wasn't my fault."

DuPont didn't always believe that. They have a 1915 safety manual that contains an analysis of injuries that lists 25.9% as unavoidable (2.1% physical deficiency, 0.9% act of God—the ultimate in finger pointing, and 22.9% as inherent in industrial employment). But since then they have investigated thousands of incidents and their findings have been that there is *always* a cause, that the cause is *always* within their control, and that there is *always* a way to prevent reoccurrence.

Our External category is like the unavoidable injury—"It's not my fault." Choosing External almost certainly means that you have not asked the Five Why questions carefully enough.

Pareto Analysis

How many of you know what *pareto* means? Better yet, how many know who Mr. Pareto was? He was an Italian economist who made the observation that 80% of the wealth resided in 20% of the population. Others later generalized that into the 80/20 rule; 80% of anything resides in 20% of the population. You get 80% of your business from 20% of your customers, 80% of grievances from 20% of employees, 80% of your kisses from 20% of your beaus.

The act of "paretoizing" is no more than grouping your causes to find the 20% of causes that create 80% of your failures. (Remember, *failure* here refers to failure to meet the objective Takt Rate.)

Our cause categories have almost done the pareto work for us; all we have to do is ask the why questions and then plot out the result.

A typical pareto chart is shown in Figure 20.1. Here, complaint causes are displayed (each bar represents a particular cause). The focus logic is that we'll want to pick out the two to three biggest causes (as our fat rabbits) and attack those first. The chart is nothing more than a convenient, effective way of presenting the information to management and getting their focus concurrence.

Notice the flow of information here; it is a critical Time concept:

- Goal takt was set for the floor.
- The floor monitored performance and noted the problems.

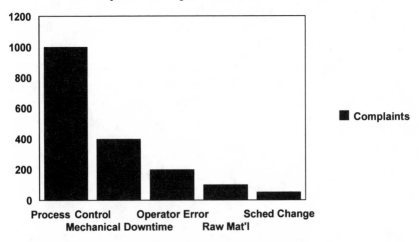

Figure 20.1   A Typical Pareto Chart

- The floor converted problems to causes.
- The floor identified the key causes and funneled those few up to management.
- Management provided resources to eliminate those causes.

Notice what *didn't* happen. Management did not decide what the floor needed to do and then direct that action; they listened and then responded. The only thing left to do is correct the problem.

Problem Correction

We now have the fat rabbit in our sights; the only thing left to do is kill it, eat it, and only then look around for another. Refer back to the safety example of a correction hierarchy: training and procedures, guarding, and permanent elimination. In the safety world, world-class practitioners think from elimination toward training. We want to eliminate, will reluctantly settle for guarding, and only as an unavoidable last resort accept training. The great unwashed think in reverse; they grab on to training, rarely guard, and almost never eliminate.

Manufacturing improvement is just the same. Once we've focused on a key cause, we want to eliminate it, not just learn to live with it. The TQM tools discussed in Section 3 will probably come into play here. SPC and TPM are good examples of elimination tools. SQC— testing and then reacting—is an equivalent to the second level in the safety hierarchy, guarding. Working on procedures, operating instructions, and so on is the equivalent of safety's first level, training. Management's response to the problem pareto information funneling up to them leads us to the topic of the next chapter, structuring the management process.

CHAPTER 21

Management Structure

The problem/cause analysis we've created begs for a management structure to make logical and effective use of that information flow. You'll want to review all your regular meetings and decision-making processes. You'll find them confusing and redundant, and you'll want to simplify the management process in the same way you've simplified the manufacturing process.

You might even map the management process in the same way we went through the manufacturing operation in Section 3. Or you might just start from scratch and create a new management structure. Yours should be designed for you, but Figure 21.1 shows a typical structure. We'll discuss each of these components.

Shift Change

The purpose of the shift change meeting is simply to maintain continuity in the operation as the crews change off. The Takt Board be-

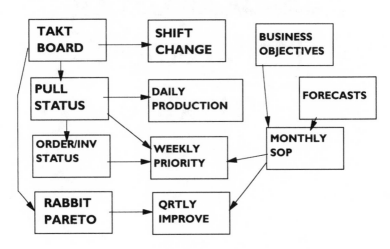

Figure 21.1   A Time-Driven Management System

comes the focal point for those discussions, as it contains all the criti-cal elements: what are we trying to do, what are we actually doing, what are the problems, who is fixing them, and what are the kanban statuses?

Our general former practice was for the off-going supervisor to fill out a shift change report and hold the discussions in the supervisor's office. With Visible Management (and Takt Boards) the discussion moved out into the work area and came to involve the hourly workers (talk about *empowerment* by *involvement*). In fact, some plants that I've worked with are trying to flatten the organization and move toward self-managed work teams. Nothing helps that process like making the operation visible.

One issue is the loss of the printed record; what replaces the file of shift change reports? That is a real problem, and I offer these com-ments.

- One option is to take a Polaroid of the board.
- A close alternative is to use a whiteboard—the Teflon-surfaced board that can be written on with a dry-erase marker and can then be copied onto an 8½-by-11-inch sheet.
- A better alternative may be to ask "How often did we ever *look* at the report file?"

Daily Production Meeting

The typical plant has a regular morning meeting to go over the plant status, review the night's results, and to plan actions for the day. The typical questions asked and answered in the production meeting are:

- What are the current operating problems? (yields, runnability, mechanical problems)
- What are the current customer order issues? Do we have any critical delays? Do we have any emergency new orders?
- What are today's emergency/unscheduled maintenance needs?
- What kinds of technical/process assistance do we need from the process engineers?

Typically, this meeting is focused on the very short term: "What do we need to do *today*?" (Other meetings within this structure deal with longer-range issues.)

PULL STATUS

Status of the Pull System goes a long way toward answering the questions of the daily meeting. *Status* refers to:

- What are the kanban statuses? Remember, we built kanbans with management alarms: Which are in danger of filling up and causing us to slow up or shut down, which are in danger of running empty?
- If we're using a production wheel, is it on time? Is it running behind, such that we are going to be late starting upcoming campaigns? Is it running ahead, giving us options for inserting special cases into the schedule?

If you know that status, you've gone a long way toward knowing your immediate priorities. Do we have time to take optional maintenance? Do we need to work overtime to get that machine back, or do we have a cushion? Can we take this special customer request? Are we going to succeed in expediting this delayed order?

In our prior experience, these decisions got made by emotion or by who shouted loudest. With tools like the Takt Board and status of the Pull System, we shifted to management by fact and by logic. (It is important to note that this shift to fact and logic is not always popular. To people who held sway by force of their personality or by the power of their position, this shift can be *very* threatening and uncomfortable. It is the wise Steering Team that anticipates and protects against the damage that a threatened member can inflict.)

Weekly Priorities Meeting

This meeting may be a stand-alone meeting, or it can be a special version of the daily production meeting. Whereas the daily meeting looks at what needs to be done to survive that day, the weekly meeting looks at where we are relative to the monthly objectives and revises the plan over the next week to maintain or get back onto the monthly projection.

Decisions/topics for this meeting include:

- Scheduled maintenance for the upcoming week. (This meeting may be a stand-alone meeting.)
- Research/test schedules for the week. This can/will include revisions in assignments of technical or support people.
- Special revisions or insertions in the normal production plan.
- Response to any special marketing/sales opportunities.

The basis for these decisions comes from the status of production/inventory.

PRODUCTION AND INVENTORY STATUS

As the weekly meeting is an extension of the daily, these data are an extension of the Pull Status.

Pull Status gave us a view of the kanbans, the wheel positions, and the alarms on at that point in time. The Production/Inventory Status adds:

- Month-to-date production versus SOP plan (see the following discussion)
- Month-to-date sales versus SOP
- Test/research progress versus monthly plan
- Special inventory programs outside normal kanban structure (inventory build for upcoming shutdown, for example)
- Special marketing/sales opportunity

You'll want to develop a formal report format so that information can be collected and summarized for weekly review. As with the daily meeting, you'll find that once you formalize the agenda and the presentation of status, the decisions will come easily.

Monthly Sales and Operations Planning (SOP) Meeting

This is one of the backbone meetings, the literal start of the planning process and the connection point between the business planning process (MRP) and shop-floor execution methods (Time).

Membership in SOP is the business team itself. Representatives of all business facets—manufacturing, sales and marketing, research and development, warehousing and distribution—attend and participate. Box 21.1 discusses meeting attendance and location.

The objective of SOP is nothing short of a rolling 12-month business plan, a review of accomplishment against the plan, and the forum for identifying the barriers to accomplishment that need to be removed. The agenda for each meeting includes the following:

- A review of previous month performance against the plan, including reasons for deviation from the plan

---

Box 21.1 An SOP Caveat

Attendance at an SOP meeting needs to be face-to-face. Speaker phones or video conferencing are not adequate for this foundational planning function.

Rotate the meeting location to spread the inconvenience or cost. The small travel expense will be richly repaid in a more integrated business team, more dynamic business plans, and ultimately a continually strengthening competitive position.

- A revision and extension of the 12-month plan, including
  Sales by month
  Production by month
  Scheduled maintenance
  Plant capacities by month
  Inventory by month
  Market share position and identification of the limiter to share
  Research and development goals
- A detailed plan for the immediate month, including
  Takt Rate exiting the plant
  Test/development schedules
  Scheduled maintenance or shutdown allowances

This may seem like a daunting set of objectives, and you may be envisioning a two-day meeting. At the start, that may be so. But, like the other meetings we've described, a preset agenda and a format for collecting and presenting the needed data goes a long way toward simplifying this meeting.

After a short start-up period filled with growing pains, you'll find yourself with a well-thought-out plan, and each month will only involve fine-tuning and adjusting to the unexpected. A good SOP meeting can be held in under two hours.

Quarterly Continuous Improvement Meeting

This brings us to the last in this meeting structure. If the SOP meeting is the foundation for the business team, this meeting is the foundation for the plant's health and growth. To give you the basis for the structure that I recommend, I need to tell you a story from my early cycle time experience (see Box 21.2). The moral of the story should be obvious; the only effective focus is *extreme* focus. In my travels since Du Pont, I've seen the same thing that we learned inside Du Pont: Organizations don't have a clue concerning focus; they try to fix everything and thereby fix nothing.

I strongly recommend you adopt your own version of the preceding policy: a severe limitation on the number of problems that you choose to attack at any one time and no option to churn the selection list. To get something new onto the active list, you must first fix something already on the list. With that policy firmly established, you'll be very careful about what you do put on your active list.

Before we discuss details of the quarterly improvement meeting, I want to first touch on the issue of *technical assistance versus process assistance.* How do you manage assignments concerning long-term development and immediate line assistance (read as fire fighting)? Most organizations tend to view development as the more desirable or more prestigious assignment, are reluctant to refuse anyone a piece of the pie, and so end up giving everyone a split long-term and short-term mix of assignments. In my experience, there is a fundamental flaw in that approach, as noted in Box 21.3.

My point is simple: You can't be expected to devote any significant attention to long-term objectives if your today is going to be damaged. As soon as I've been woken up a few times, or been dragged away from my family, I'm going to learn that I darn well better make sure that the shop's immediate needs are taken care of. And I'm going to develop negative assumptions about even starting any long-term work.

Box 21.2 A Focus Example

In one of our very first Du Pont experiences, we were excited with the idea of empowering the floor to identify the detractors. We did such a good job of turning people on to that idea, we literally papered the walls of the plant with problems; we drowned in them. As you can imagine, we couldn't settle on any direction, didn't fix anything, and disenchanted everyone.

In our next plant, we said "We better learn to focus," so we limited ourselves to the top 10 problems (or rabbits; remember our analogy of chasing rabbits in a field). People looked at the list and said "Yup ... you've got that right. Those problems have been around forever; if you fix those, we'll really fly!"

When we checked two months later, we still had those 10 problems. When we checked two more months later, we *still* had those 10 problems.

We then said, "We've *really* got to learn to focus!" And we set two rigid rules:

- We will concentrate on only *three* problems.
- We will *not* change our mind; the only way to get a problem off the list is to *fix* it. We can't put a new one on without taking an old one off.

Only then did we make progress on our list.

Box 21.3 Long-Term vs. Short-Term: A Fundamental Problem

If I think my phone may ring at 2:00 A.M.
    Then I'll do everything to keep that from happening!

My recommendation is simple and obvious: Don't mix these assignments. You may need to rotate these assignments to keep everyone happy, and you'll need to work on your performance evaluation methods so that people's peer rankings don't suffer. But you'll see improvement in *both* long- and short-term programs if you keep them separate.

So we'll assume that short-term assistance includes fire fighting, operating standards and instructions, and very short-term customer or product test work. This work is monitored and directed in the daily and weekly meetings discussed earlier. Long-term technical development of a fundamental nature is managed in the quarterly improvement meeting.

THE "RABBIT" PARETO

This analogy was referred to earlier: If you're going to catch a rabbit, you need to pick out the biggest, fattest, slowest rabbit and then chase, catch, and eat that rabbit before you even look at the others. Problems are just like that; which few are we going to be *absolutely sure* that we catch?

To keep the analogy in front of us, I'll refer to our chosen problems as our rabbits. We've already discussed how we're going to pick out our rabbits in Chapter 20. We talked about the process of capturing detractors on the Takt Board, reducing them to root causes, and paretoizing those root causes to find the few that are most significant.

This quarterly meeting is nothing more than the formal meeting that recognizes that process, that makes the assignment of rabbits and monitors progress of the hunt. Box 21.4 lists some summary guidelines for this meeting. A little guidance on completion dates—don't dictate them to the assignees. It's much better to let people select their own objectives, even if you may think they're not aggressive. You don't get ownership and buy-in by dictating; you'll only get a self-fulfilling prophecy as people work to show you that your imposed objectives weren't fair.

You may question why this meeting only happens quarterly: What if things change in the interim? If you're concerned about what to do if

---

**Box 21.4   Guidelines: Quarterly
             Improvement Meeting**

- A strict limitation on the number of rabbits.
- No changing your mind on rabbit selection.
- Pareto rabbit list prepared by the floor and funneled upward.
- Resources aimed at the fat rabbits flow back out.
- No mixing of fire fighting and rabbit chasing.
    —Rotate assignments to keep everyone happy.
    —Keep performance evaluations fair to all.
- Good project management skills.
    —Specify by-name assignments.
    —Clear program objectives.
    —Expected completion dates.

---

problems are resolved, you have the pareto list and can automatically shift to the next one on the list. If you're concerned about priorities changing, you don't have the right view of priority setting, as priorities just don't change that fast. If you're changing priorities faster than once per quarter, you're not being rigorous enough about your priority evaluation.

Summary

We'll end this section the same way we began. To build or revise your own management structure, you'll want to map your meetings and decision process the same way you mapped your manufacturing process. Lay out the management activities you need to attend to, the meetings on your regular schedule, and then *simplify*. Create a management structure map like the one suggested earlier in this section (or just use that one) and then challenge any additional meetings or complexity.

Box 21.5   What Constitutes a
Well-Planned Meeting?

- A planned agenda
- A specific attendee list, including consideration for:
  —Sending substitutes
  —Attending by phone or video conference
- An established meeting date and time
- A time objective for conducting the meeting (resist anything over 1.5 hr)
- A standard format for input information
- Clear expectation for output of the meeting

Box 21.5 contains a checklist for building the structure of each meeting in your (new) management system. A couple of comments on this checklist:

- Attendance: I recommend a very tight attendance list, with the provision that attendance to observe is open (and encouraged) to anyone. For the SOP and improvement meetings, I recommend no substitutions (except for vacations) and personal attendance at the meeting (no conference calls). These two meetings are too critical for anything less than full commitment.
- Time objectives. You may choke on the idea of one- to one-and-a-half-hour meeting limits. We're all familiar with meetings that drag on all day. You may have problems particularly with the first SOP meetings; they can be very difficult if you are not in the habit of addressing these core issues. But this is what preplanning and standard formats are for. All meetings except SOP should be accomplishable in *no more* than one hour, and SOP should be limited to two hours, tops.

CHAPTER 22

The Benchmarks

We've finished each section in this book with a checklist to assure us that we have satisfactorily completed the work of that segment. This final section, however, does not include a completion checklist, because *you never finish continuous improvement!* It is an ongoing journey that never ends. We do finish with a self-evaluation of your status compared with the way a world-class company conducts itself on that endless journey.

Our benchmark is comprised of seven segments. A perfect score of 10 in all 7 segments doesn't mean that you're done, it means you're growing as fast and as broadly as is possible. Keep coming back to the overall benchmark and work on getting faster.

The Time Benchmark

The overall Time benchmark recognizes three "states of grace" (see Figure 22.1). *Evolving* refers to the basic, or fundamental, underpin-

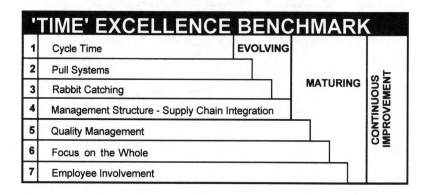

Figure 22.1 The Overall Time Benchmark

nings of pursuing a cycle time strategy and of driving continuous improvement. Some level of progress in four of the seven evaluation categories is required to be considered as Evolving. *Maturing* describes a more elevated capability and some progress in all seven categories is required. *Continuous Improvement* is true world class and defines a state where full maturity in all categories has been achieved.

Note again that even a continuous improvement state does not mean you are done. It only means that you are growing, learning, evolving, and maturing at an optimum rate. You'll keep on keeping on, *forever*.

CYCLE TIME: THE PRIME METRIC

Obviously, Cycle Time is the foundation for this process and is the driver for everything else. The benchmark standard in Figure 22.2 should be self-explanatory, with a few exceptions.

- MCE refers to Manufacturing Cycle Efficiency and is the ratio of Value-Add Time (the time when the product is actually being altered or processed in a way that the customer would value and pay for, excluding all waiting, testing, reworking, sorting, etc.) to Cycle Time.
- Significant reduction in Cycle Time would relate to the MCE starting point. For the process industry, MCE's of less than 1% to

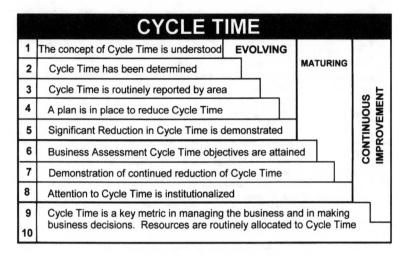

Figure 22.2 Benchmarking Cycle Time Status

2% are common in unimproved operations, while 10% to 15% may be absolute world class. So, moving from 1% to 3% MCE might be significant.

- Business Assessment refers to the improvement plan you put together at the end of Section 3.
- Institutionalized Cycle Time would mean that this metric is ingrained in the culture and the business management process and is no longer "program de jour."

PULL SCHEDULING SYSTEMS: THE PRIMARY TIME TOOL

Pull Scheduling is the foundation of operating under a cycle time concept. Remember that Pull Systems, in themselves, don't improve the operation. Pull only allows you to run effectively at the minimum Cycle Time given your current capability. Secondarily, analysis of Pull necessities allow one to be selective about what needs to be improved.

State #6 (see Figure 22.3) refers to analyzing the Pull System structure and the Cycle Time that is resident within it, and understanding what the few biggest improvement opportunities are. (Focus!)

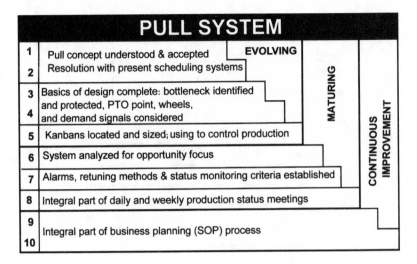

Figure 22.3 Evaluating Pull Status

FOCUSED IMPROVEMENT: THE PATH FORWARD

Achieving a concept of focus is absolutely critical (see Figure 22.4). You won't really begin making progress until you learn to be astutely

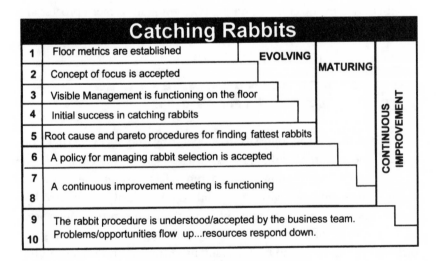

Figure 22.4 The Rabbit Benchmark

selective. Being selective or focused is based on the idea of performance metrics. If you know in a very focused way *what* you want to improve, you can then be selective about what you *are*, and *are not*, going to pursue. Your approach will include a specific policy about how many opportunities you can afford to pursue at any one time and some commitment to not change your mind or churn the program. Employee involvement and commitment is fostered by the fact that opportunities are identified by the shop floor and flow upward to management for resolution. (Too often, it is management that is deciding for and dictating to the shop floor; that approach doesn't empower or build ownership.)

INTEGRATING BUSINESS COMPONENTS

This benchmark (see Figure 22.5) describes the structure in place for both managing the daily operation and for driving long-range continuous improvement. Meetings have been carefully structured, have well-defined agendas and time limits, and attendance rules are in place. Attendees understand how the meeting in progress fits into the larger

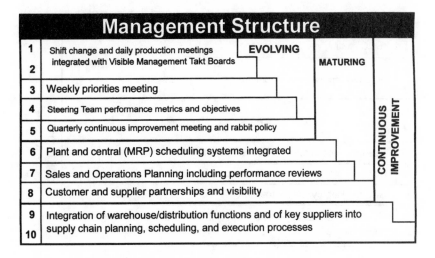

Figure 22.5 Benchmarking Management Systems

scheme. Participation is respectful and supportive. All meetings are open for all interested parties to attend and monitor.

Building Quality

The objective within this benchmark is to move quality management toward the floor (see Figure 22.6). You *measure* quality in the lab, but you *manage* quality where it is made.

The benchmark mandates a partnership with your customers, which implies that your vendors will forge partnerships with you as well, that this extended partnership recognizes that competition within the alliance (a win/lose approach to the relationship) will detract from everyone in the partnership.

The final state describes an environment where specs are set to *true* customer need, the partner understands the value of not pushing beyond those specs, the process is so well defined that its operating conditions to deliver those specs are clearly defined, and that process is monitored and managed on the floor in real time, with a clear distinction between internal and external causes for deviation.

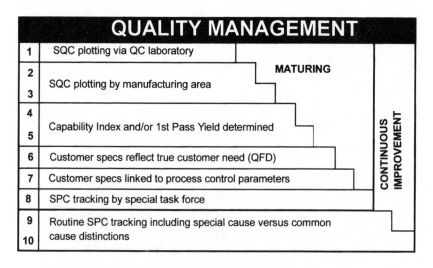

Figure 22.6 Benchmarking Quality

AVOIDING LOCAL OPTIMIZATION— CONCENTRATING ON THE OVERALL

Local optimization and area competition have been banished (see Figure 22.7). Everyone understands the objective for the whole, understands their contribution to the larger whole, has personal metrics that relate to the whole, and makes local sacrifice to better the whole. Performance evaluations and compensation reflect value for optimizing the larger whole.

EMPOWERMENT

The final, and perhaps the most important, benchmark (see Figure 22.8) defines the state of efforts to engage the shop floor in this crusade. It defines a state where everyone understands their role, values their ability to contribute, and is valued for their contributions. People don't "park their brains at the door" but contribute to their own maximum. People are linked together, rigid area boundaries are gone. Management leads and defines strategy, and the floor defines the most important opportunities and tactics toward achievement of those strategies.

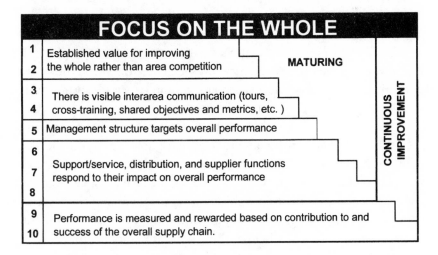

Figure 22.7 Going for the Whole

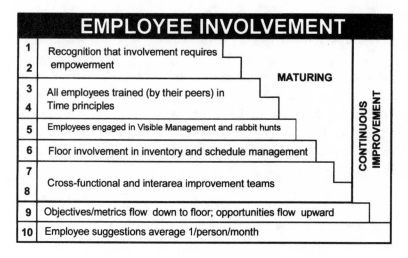

Figure 22.8   Measuring Employee Involvement

Conclusion

Throughout this book, I've continually posed the question "How will we know when we're done?" In every prior case I've defined what finished that section and then moved on to a new task. This time, we are truly done with this Time project, but we'll never be done using the tools we've put in place to continue improvement.

I've walked through this process—live—with many people, and I've always enjoyed the experience. To see people discover a new way of thinking and to see their delight at the simplicity and power of this paradigm is always fulfilling.

Now, as I am writing these last lines before anyone has actually used this book, I am writing in anticipation of how arriving at the end point of this process will feel ... for you and for me. From my point of view, I'm gratified to know that this book will make it possible for many company teams to benefit from this process, without having to depend on Process/Time Management being with you. I'm satisfied with the effort, because I know I've held nothing back: If you follow the process, with rigor and discipline, you cannot fail! In fact, if you have truly followed the process with discipline, you can't have even gotten to this point without doing the work. You have done a *ton* of very good work to get here, and I know that you have extracted major benefits for your company and for your customers.

My regret is that I didn't get to take the journey with you. If I had, I know I would have learned as much as you; I only built this process by experiencing the work with my clients and friends. My fear is that the availability of this book will end my own personal learning process. So let me assure you that, whether we have worked directly together or have worked together only through this book, I consider you more than a business associate; I consider you a personal friend. And I hope that relationship will continue. Please consider yourself a Process/Time Management associate or partner: I hope you'll contact me, whether to share your experience and learning or to ask a question.

My sincere thanks for this experience and my best wishes for your continuing journey.

Questions or comments may be directed to:
Process/Time Management
West Chester, PA 19382
http://www.ptma.com
ptma@ptma.com

Notes

1. Dr. Joel Barker, *The Power of The Paradigm* (New York: Harper Business, 1993).
2. "Manufacturing Resource Planning." See Section 3, Chapter 15.
3. "Statistical Quality Control." See Chapter 15.
4. "Statistical Process Control." A significant advance over SQC. See Chapter 15.
5. "Quality Function Deployment." Inserting the voice of the customer into process/product design. Chapter 15.
6. "Total Productive Maintenance." Chapter 15.
7. "Management Information Systems."
8. Dr. Eli Goldratt, *The Goal* (Croton-on-Hudson, NY: Twin Rivers Press, 1985).
9. "Six Sigma" refers to the quality standard created by Motorola. It refers to quality standards that reflect true customer needs and that describe a range that is twice the actual product quality variability, plus/minus six standard deviations compared to the plus/minus three standard deviations that would encompass essentially (99.7%) all product output. It describes a capability state where conformance to the voice of the customer is ensured.
10. Many texts deal with the concept of Pull; see the bibliography. The work that describes the initial Pull implementation is *The Toyota Production System* by Taiichi Ohno. (Cambridge: Productivity Press, 1988).

11. Inspired by Robert Kaplan and David Norton, *The Balanced Scorecard* (Boston: Harvard Business Press, 1996). Although the authors define four specific strategic areas, we are more flexible and encourage businesses to define for themselves the four corners of their own playing field. What is important is that managers think broadly about all aspects of their environment and their strategies within each "corner" of that environment.

12. Also known as a "Triple Diagonal Model." See Joseph Montgomery and Lawrence Levine, *The Transition to Agile Manufacturing* (Milwaukee: ASQC Quality Press, 1996).

13. One good example is *"Extend"* offered by Imagine That, Inc. See Section 3 for details.

14. A good handbook on the Seven Management Tools is offered by The American Supplier Institute (Dearborn, MI).

15. Contact Goal/QPC (Methuen, MA) for their excellent pocket handbook on these fundamental techniques.

16. Although heavily slanted to discrete parts, see Charles Snead, *Group Technology: Foundation for Competitive Manufacturing* (New York: Van Nostrand Reinhold, 1989)

17. See Gwendolyn Galsworth Visual Systems (New York: Amacom Press, 1997).

18. See Shrikanth and Umble, *Synchronous Manufacturing* (Cincinnati: South-Western Publishing, 1987) for a complete discussion of this critical observation.

19. *SMED*, Productivity Press, 1984.

20. See Thomas A. Stewart, *Intellectual Capital* (New York: Doubleday/Currency, 1997.)

21. See Joseph Montgomery and Lawrence Levine, *The Transition to Agile Manufacturing* (Milwaukee: ASQC Quality Press, 1996).

22. Contact The American Supplier Institute (Dearborn, Michigan) for an excellent and brief handbook.

Bibliography

Recommended reading in advanced manufacturing techniques:

Barker, Joel. *The Power of the Paradigm*. New York: Harper Business, 1993. The difficulty in adapting to new perspectives.

Deming, W. Edwards. *Out of Crisis*. Cambridge: MIT Center for Advanced Engineering, 1986. The landmark book on quality management.

Ford, Henry. *Today and Tomorrow*. Garden City: Garden City Publishing, 1926. Ford laid out the foundation for cycle time, but we didn't listen!

Galsworth, Gwendolyn D. *Visual Systems*. Amacom Press, 1996. An excellent workbook for creating visible shop floor management systems.

Goldratt, Eliyahu M., and Jeff Cox. *The Goal*, revised edition. Croton-on-Hudson: North River Press, 1987. This is a *must* read for anyone interested in breaking out of old manufacturing paradigms. Buy a copy for everyone on your team.

Kaplan, Robert S., and Norton, David P. *The Balanced Scorecard*. Boston: Harvard Business Press, 1996. A definitive work on strategy, tactics, and performance measurement.

Montgomery, Joseph C., and Levine, Lawrence O., editors. *The Transition to Agile Manufacturing*. Milwaukee: ASQC Quality Press, 1996.

Moody, Patricia E., editor. *National Association of Manufacturers: Leading Manufacturing Excellence, A Guide to State-of-the-Art Manufacturing*, revised edition. New York: John Wiley and Sons, 1997. This author and Pull Systems are included.

Northey, Patrick and Southway, Nigel. *Cycle Time Management*. Portland: Productivity Press, 1993.

Ohno, Taiichi. *The Toyota Production System: Beyond Large Scale Production*. Cambridge: Productivity Press, 1988. A translation from the Japanese. Of historical importance as this depicts the introductory effort in Pull Scheduling.

Shonberger, Richard J. *World Class Manufacturing*. New York: The Free Press, 1986.

Snead, Charles. *Group Technology: The Foundation for Competitive Advantage*. New York: Van Nostrand Reinhold Publishing, 1989. Although heavily slanted toward discrete parts, an excellent introduction to the topic of controlling and simplifying routes through the plant.

Srikanth, Mokshagundam. *Synchronous Manufacturing*. Cincinnati: South-West Publishing, 1990. The first work to recognize the problem of divergence.

For a perspective on more traditional methods:

Landvater, Darryl V. *World Class Production & Inventory Control*. New York: John Wiley & Sons, 1993.

Wight, Oliver. *MRP II: Unlocking America's Productivity Potential*. Boston: CBI Publishing, 1987. To work within (and to understand) MRP systems, this is the book.

For important supporting perspectives:

Byham, William C. *Zapp: The Lighting of Empowerment*. New York: Harmony Books, 1990. In the end, everything happens through people.

Stewart, Thomas A. *Intellectual Capital*. New York: Doubleday/Currency, 1997. The increasing strategic value of knowledge held and the importance of dispersing and leveraging that knowledge through the organization.

Index